MW01032406

CONTENTS

Labor

IN CHAINS

"THE DANGEROUS WORLD OF HUMAN TRAFFICKING"

Co-Authored by:

Alan R. Warren, PhD

RJ Parker, PhD

ISBN-13: 978-1987902624

ISBN-10: 1987902629

Copyrights

APPRECIATION

Much gratitude to our editor and cover design, Evening Sky Publishing Services, and to our beta-readers; Rebecca Coulter, and Kathi Garcia

Alan R. Warren

BOOK DESCRIPTION

Human trafficking is the trade of people for forced labor or sex. It also includes the illegal extraction of human organs and tissues. And it is an extremely ruthless and dangerous industry plaguing our world today.

Most believe human trafficking occurs in countries with no human rights legislation. This is a myth. All types of human trafficking are alive and well in most of the developed countries of the world like the United States, Canada, and the UK. It is estimated that $150 billion a year is generated in the forced labor industry alone. It is also believed that 21 million people are trapped in modern day slavery – exploited for sex, labor, or organs.

Most also believe since they live in a free country, there is built-in protection against such illegal practices. But for many, this is not the case. Traffickers tend to focus on the most vulnerable in our society, but trafficking can happen to anyone. You will see how easy it can happen in the stories included in "In Chains."

4

INTRODUCTION

As we were finishing this book, news broke that Robert Kraft was arrested and charged with two counts of soliciting prostitution. The charges resulted from a string of arrests on massage parlors in Jupiter, Florida, which according to the Palm Beach state attorney's office, were used for prostitution and human trafficking.

For those that don't know who Robert Kraft is, he is the chairman and chief executive officer of The Kraft Group - a diversified holding company with assets in paper, packaging, sports, and entertainment. Kraft himself owns the NFL's New England Patriots, and Major League's Soccer team The New England Revolution, as well as the Gillette Stadium that both teams play in. Kraft was allegedly videotaped while involved in sexual activity with the female masseuse. The spokesperson for Kraft denied that he engaged in any illegal activity.

Investigators suspected that the managers of a day spa were trafficking the women working there, forcing them to perform sex acts on their clients. The state attorney announced to the media that there would be a total of 25 people charged with first-degree misdemeanors for soliciting prostitution.

Robert Kraft is a billionaire, and even if he is convicted of these charges, he only faces a maximum of 120 days in county jail. At the time the incident took place, Kraft was a resident of another state, Massachusetts, not Florida where the spa was located. Misdemeanors such as these are not extraditable offenses. A further report was released to the press claiming that Kraft was not even the biggest name to be involved in the scandal, or to be arrested.

According to Attorney Stewart Ryan, who handled several cases like this for the Montgomery County District Attorney's Office says, *"The purpose of such large-scale busts are to shut it down at the top level, as opposed to just going in and arresting people on prostitution charges, and then the shop moves down the street and opens up again a week later."*

Ryan also claims, *"It is not uncommon for such large-scale prostitution cases to also involve charges of human trafficking, as the people brought in to work, sometimes from another country, come with the understanding something very different than they end up doing, and find themselves working under brutal conditions with few options for recourse or escape."*

At this point, Kraft doesn't even have to appear in court to face the charges. He can appoint an attorney from Florida, and they will file a notice of representation on his behalf. That will ensure Kraft has retained legal counsel, and the counsellor will represent him in court. Most likely, there will be a plea agreement of some money, and no trial or jail time.

The owner of this particular spa in Jupiter, Hua Zhang, was arrested and charged with sex trafficking. He was just one of 11 arrested. Detective Snyder, an investigator working this case, claims that they have followed as much as $20 million going in and out of China from this business. And Florida ranks third in the United States for the number of human trafficking cases that have been reported.

In this trafficking operation, most of the women were brought to the United States from China under the guise of having legitimate jobs in the spa. Most of them believed they were going to work there legitimately when they arrived. They soon found themselves forced to work in the sex trade, and confined to sleeping and eating in the same place they were working. Quite often in these types of operations, all of the victims live in one or two rooms, with only a kitchen and dresser in their place. They stay in their room at all times except when they are working in the massage rooms. They are trapped there until they can pay off the debt their captors say they owe for being brought to the United States. The amount due is usually inflated, and the victims are only given pennies on the dollar of what the men pay for sex.

Here's where things get very complicated. When it comes to these situations, law enforcement can arrest and charge the women as well. The law states that if they were in the US working illegally, they could be arrested. And it does happen, quite often, that victims of human trafficking are arrested. So, if these women who were smuggled into the US from China are charged with participating in criminal activity, they will be subject to prosecution and deportation. Instead, if they are designated as human trafficking victims, they are eligible for a "T visa," which was created in 2000 specifically for human trafficking victims.

According to Sarah Paoletti, Director of the University of Pennsylvania Law School's International Human Rights and Immigration Clinic, the road from being rescued by law enforcement to getting residency in the United States is a very long one. Police will either treat them as trafficking victims or as prostitutes. It's possible they could end up as criminals rather than victims. Unfortunately, the criminal route happens quite often.

The T Visa was created in October of 2000, and according to U.S. Citizenship and Immigration Services, only 5,000 are available each year. Typically, victims of sex trafficking don't have the money to secure any legal advice or attorneys. Without the resources of human rights organizations, these victims fall through the cracks and end up with a conviction, and later deported back to their country of origin. Since the passage of the T Visa law, there have only been between 7,000 and 9,000 of these visas granted in total -   roughly 500 per year - much less than the 5,000 available.

So, at the end of a great sting such as the recent one in Florida, most of the men that bought the massage with a sexual ending, will only end up with a misdemeanor charge, pay a fine, and go about their lives. The wealthy, high profile men such as Robert Kraft, will walk away with no conviction, and a small fine. The workers (and most likely trafficking victims) will be prosecuted for prostitution and deported with no money to start over in China. Even though that particular spa will be closed, several more will open down the road soon enough.

After the newspapers and television media move on to the next big story, human trafficking will still go on the same as it did before, only with new faces in the mix.

PART ONE: THE DANGEROUS WORLD OF HUMAN TRAFFICKING

CHAPTER 1: SEX TRAFFICKING

If you think sex trafficking only happens in third world countries, then think again. An example of how sex trafficking can happen right here at home was outlined in a New York Times article from April 12, 2012, by Nicholas Kristof. In this article, Kristof interviewed a 16-year-old girl he called 'Brianna' to protect her real identity.

Brianna grew up in New York City, in an average middle-class family, with two parents and an older brother. She claims that it all started when she was 12 years old. She fought with her mother and ended up going over to her friend's house.

Brianna was scared to go home and thought she was in big trouble. Being a young teenage girl and looking for support, she told all her friends about what happened. A friend's older brother told Brianna she could stay at his place until things cooled down at home if she wanted. Brianna took him up on his offer, figuring she would go home the next morning. She thought that staying away all night would teach her mother a lesson for yelling at her.

When Brianna woke up the next morning, she used the bathroom, quickly got ready, and told her friend's brother it was time that she went home. But then, things got ugly. The man said she couldn't go home, and according to him, she was now his property. He told her that he was a pimp and he now owned her.

The man physically forced Brianna into a bedroom and locked the door. He would enter the bedroom about every two hours or so. The first time he entered he beat her, pushed her around, and called her bad names. The next time he came in he was just the opposite, showing her great affection. The man kept up this back and forth abusive behavior for a couple of days before he started selling her to men for sex.

Brianna remembers her captor saying more than half of the men came from an ad the man placed on the Internet site, Backpage.com. At the time, Backpage was responsible for about 70% of the prostitution ads placed in the United States. In response to this, Backpage claimed as far as they were concerned, many of the ads in their paper and website, were placed by consenting adults, and not traffickers. In early 2018, the FBI shut down Backpage, so it no longer operates. However, in the world of the Internet, there are plenty of other places for the ads to go. When one site like Backpage is shut down, the ads just move to another site.

Brianna ended up at Gateways Treatment

Center in Pleasantville, about 35 miles from New York, and this is where she felt safe enough to tell some of her story. Gateways is one of many treatment centers meant for girls between the ages of 12 and 16, that have survived being used as a sexual slave by a trafficker or a pimp. Brianna continued her story by telling the reporter that when she was held captive, she was afraid of being killed, or beaten severely if she tried to run away. Going to the police wasn't an option either, as she figured she would be arrested and sent to jail. Brianna remembers one time when she was looking out the bedroom window from where she was being held captive. She saw her mother walking the street in front of the house where she was held. She screamed through the window and started slapping the window with her hand. The pimp came from out of nowhere, grabbed her by throat, told her to shut up, or he would kill her.

Quite often the girls that have been forced into the sex slave trade end up staying. Not only out of fear of their captors but also because they develop affection for the captor. This is widely known as "Stockholm Syndrome."

In an odd twist of fate, Backpage was actually a valuable resource for local police to find victims. Often, a pimp would place a picture of the girl they were selling, and police would contact the ad pretending to be interested in purchasing the girl. They'd make arrangements, and when they got the girl to safety, they arrested the pimp. Since the FBI put Backpage out of business, it's no longer a resource that can be used.

Crysta Price and Terry Clark have spent over two years running the Creighton University's Human Trafficking Initiative, which uses scientific data gleaned from websites that help sell people. Their work is supporting law enforcement to understand the commercial sex industry by identifying who is involved, and how often people are trafficked.

It was Creighton that focused their analysis on the website Backpage. They stated, at any given time, there were dozens of ads with pictures showing girls in sexually provocative positions offering their services. The ads even included the prices they charged for those services. They provided an array of services for many sexual appetites, including everything from bondage, S&M, to quick encounters. Backpage was considered the primary site for the commercial sex industry.

Price said, *"I'm absolutely not convinced that a website being shut down suddenly will make traffickers say, 'Oh okay, you guys are free to go' or 'Okay, I'm going to stop trying to exploit you simply because this one website is shut down.' They're going to find another way, and we're always going to be behind."*

"I think it's clear that the laws created chaos in this industry and that chaos is still shaking out. I don't

think anybody argued it was going to end trafficking or prostitution. It certainly hasn't." Clark said, *"The question were not sure of is, Okay, what is really the effect? Has it increased or decreased trafficking as a percentage of the entire industry? I think those are the questions that are good questions to ask, and that I don't know if we have answers to those yet."*

When a website like Backpage is taken down, the sex trade moves on to another website. You can find some examples in countries like Austria, India, and Russia. Sites like BedPage, CityX Guide, and Adult Search are doing the same thing Backpage was doing in the U.S. Only now they are out of reach of the U.S. law enforcement.

Price claims, *"It was this weird sort of shock and awe situation, almost like a panic where the new sites that then come up are sites that no one was ever looking at or watching. Their servers are not in the United States. That's how they're able to kind of get around it. They're all kind of marketing to try to get at the Backpage market, right? To capture that."*

Price believes some of the other sex websites will get close to the market share that Backpage had, and it won't be hard to find a server in one of the other countries that don't regulate against selling sex online. There's a ton of money to be made in this sort of business, so there will be at least one entrepreneur that will get behind something like this.

Alan R. Warren

"It put the power in the hands of the johns, the sex buyers who are a little bit more in control now. You've got the individuals who are either trafficked or forced by circumstance to be in the industry who still need to bring home the same quota, or their rent really still stayed the same," says Price. *"It becomes kind of a scrambling, trying to figure out how to bring home the same amount of money and how to reach the johns. The johns, if you think about it, they don't need to scramble to survive. They still want to see the girls, but it doesn't come down to survival for them."*

Bringing down a major sex-buying site like Backpage also brought lower prices for the work and a lot of specials or deals for the customers. There is also now an increase in unsafe services being offered, whereas before, they would be hard to find, not to mention very expensive. Clark told us, *"Sex without condoms would be an obvious service now offered, but that's not all. It has opened up services the sex workers would prefer not to engage in, but in order for the traffickers to make their quota, its now being offered and for a lower price. The john is in the position of power, a bargaining position that they didn't have just two years ago,"*

Law enforcement agencies fighting against human trafficking now have new challenges since the shutdown of Backpage and Craigslist services sites. In the past where the selling of sex services was centralized on Backpage, they could quickly focus on that site alone during their investigations.

16

Now, they have to watch many websites, and when they find a suspicious posting, they have to secure subpoenas for many sites. Some of them are not even in the United States. For this reason, the majority of the subpoenas are not going to get a response. This already underground industry was difficult to investigate before when it was centralized, now it is almost impossible.

While it seems counter-intuitive to discuss the negative aspects of closing a sex trafficking site like Backpage, they needed mentioning. But on the other hand, so many have been exploited on Backpage, and it's because of them that we need to do more to put an end to this industry all together. Sadly, shutting down Backpage did not end sex trafficking.

CRAIGSLIST CONFESSIONAL

This letter came from a series called 'Craigslist Confessional' by writer Helena Bala, who had been meeting people through Craigslist and documenting their stories for over two years now. Each story was written as it was told to her. The names in the letter have been changed to protect the victim from further abuse.

JOANNA M NOW IN HER 30'S

I was born in a small town in a small country in Europe. My parents are farmers with no education, and my siblings and I were also raised to work the land. We lived a very self sufficient and isolated life, we didn't have television, and I seldom came into contact with people whom I hadn't known for my whole life. Because I didn't go to school, I could not read or write.

The summer I turned 18, I met someone who claimed to be from a nearby big city. My brother intro-duced him to me. They worked together briefly. Almost immediately, he told me that he wanted to marry me, and that he would come to ask my parents' permission. In the meantime, we saw each other secretly.

He made a lot of promises, he told me that he had a job lined up overseas and that he would take good care of me and my family, and eventually take me to live with him there. He told me that he'd help me go to school so that I could learn to read and write and get a job as well. He promised that I would get to know a different life, that we would travel and go to good restaurants. I believed him. He spoke so differently from everyone around me, and it felt like he already knew so much about me, I didn't know anything. So, I let him do what he wanted. I didn't even know I was pregnant until I told one of my friends what had happened.

I kept my pregnancy a secret from my family and he and I continued to see each other. A couple of months into our relationship, he told me that he had to leave the country so that he could go and get my documents ready and the three of us (with baby) could live together abroad. He disappeared for months and at that point, rumors had started spreading. People warned my par-ents about him. My friend told my mom that I was preg-

nant with his baby. People were saying that he would take me abroad and sell me. They had heard stories of this happening to other young women. I didn't believe that he was capable of doing something like that, I don't blame myself for how naïve I was, I had no way of knowing.

When he came back, I felt vindicated. My parents put up a fight and reported him to the police, but u wasn't listening. I went with him and we were easily allowed out of the country. Abroad, we stayed with some of his relatives. He told me it was temporary, until we could get our own place. He was seldom around, and I started catching glimpses of things that unsettled me.

When our baby was born, we went to the hospital and I signed where I was told to sign. I didn't understand the language and I couldn't read anything, so I had no idea what I was doing, except I still completely trusted him and what he was telling me. When we left the hospital without the baby, he said that they were just keeping it for observation, and we could pick it up soon. I never saw my baby again, and that's when the nightmare began.

We were kept in an apartment in a nondescript building. I was with other women who were just like me, young, uneducated, abandoned by their families and lured abroad by someone they loved, two other girls by the same guy that took me. We were drugged and raped several times a day. We were sometimes beaten. We didn't have access to doctors or to the outside world. We didn't have money or possessions. We were not allowed outside without supervision. I didn't speak the language so I couldn't call for help.

Several months into it, I got really sick. I started running a fever and threw up and initially I thought that I was pregnant again. Part of me was happy in spite of the circumstances, mostly because it would probably mean a break from being prostituted. But I got my period and the illness continued. One of the older women there who helped the traffickers manage us. She checked me and told them I was finished, literally, she's not good for anything. I didn't realize it then, but she probably saved my life.

They blindfolded me and drove me around for a couple of hours. I thought they were going to kill me, take my organs, and throw me in a trash can. I was terrified. But I was pushed out of the car and I heard them drive off. Because of what the lady had said, they probably thought my organs could be contaminated, that's what I think now, but there's no way to confirm. I was later picked up by the cops. It was days before they found someone who could communicate with me. I was kept in a jail cell and I started to withdraw from the drugs. When the translator finally came, he told me that they would start to process my deportation. I was not treated for my illness or for my withdrawals.

When I got back home, I found out that my family and small community had disowned me. I was considered a dirty person, a street person. I had nowhere to turn. I walked to the nearest city and started begging for money on the street. While I was homeless, someone approached me. I told her what had happened to me and she told me it was her job to help people like me. She took me to a clinic where I got treatment. I met other women who had gone through the same exact thing as I had, almost o the letter. Most of them had escaped, a few others, like me, had been abandoned. There are so many of us and probably so many more who don't make it out alive.

CHAPTER 2: ORGAN TRAFFICKING

Organ trafficking is a reality in many parts of the world, including Indonesia, China, India, South Africa, and Brazil. Many cases have already been documented. The demand for organ transplants, especially kidney transplants, is very high, and the waiting list in the United States is very long. At the time of writing this in 2018, according to the American Transplant Foundation, there were 123,000 people on the organ donor's wait list. An average of 25 people die each day waiting for an organ transplant, and this has created a demand for more organs in any way possible, legitimate or illegal.

In 2010, 11,000 organs were obtained on the black market according to the World Health Organization (WHO). This organization claims an organ is sold every hour, each day, every day of the year. Nancy Scherper-Hughes, a professor of medical anthropology at the University of California Berkley, and co-founder and director of 'Organs Watch' said, *"Yes, the illegal organ trade is real, and it may be happening at a hospital near you."* Scherper-Hughes also calls the demand for human body parts *"insatiable."*

Unfortunately, the flow of human organs

goes from the most impoverished communities to the wealthiest estates in the United States. The UN claims that the poorest slums of the world supply kidneys to the U.S., Europe, UK, Israel, and Canada. Scherper-Hughes has tracked organs to hospitals and medical centers in New York, Los Angeles, and Philadelphia. The WHO estimates one-fifth of all transplanted kidneys, which is about 70,000, are from trafficking each year.

The United Nations (UN) is now looking into reports that ISIS, the wealthy terrorist group, may have been in the business of selling organs. Throughout history, organ trafficking during wartime was not uncommon. In wars with undisciplined armies or terrorist groups, it's even worse. Unfortunately, in these types of conflicts, there's not a lot that the UN can do afterward. One particular country or political party is not responsible and can be held accountable.

Organized crime syndicates are also involved in the organ trafficking business. They typically use any of these three methods for obtaining the organ from a person:

1. Trickery: in some cases, a patient is told they are being treated for a particular condition or sickness, and traffickers take their organ

2. Force: they coerce the person into giving up their organ

3. Purchase: the most popular method

has been to offer a large cash payout for the desired organ. Police have had several reports where the person giving the organ was supposed to get a certain amount of money but ended up with a much lower sum

After the organ is obtained, it will go to an "organ broker," who will receive anywhere from $150,000 - $200,000 for the organ. The donor most likely only received around $5,000 if anything at all. These organ brokers can go international. They are known to have connections to 'broker-friendly hospitals and clinics,' not only in the United States but other developed countries as well. In most cases, the surgeons are not directly involved in the process itself; but they ignore where the organ comes from, don't ask questions, or are just in denial.

PRICES OF BLACK-MARKET BODY PARTS

If you are curious as to how much money body parts can get you on the black-market, here is a list of the most recent values according to the Medical Transcription Organization. These prices are all in American dollars and reflect the American market:

1.   Pair of Eye Balls - $1,525

2.   Scalp - $607

3.   Skull with Teeth - $1,200

4.   Shoulder - $500

5.   Coronary Artery - $1,525

6.   Heart - $119,000

7.   Liver - $157,000

8.   Hand and Forearm - $385

9.   Pint of Blood - $337

10.   Spleen - $508

11.   Stomach - $508

12.   Small Intestine - $2,519

13.   Kidney - $262,000

Organ trafficking may sound like a science fiction movie or book, but this happens. Some people get tired of waiting on the organ transplant list. Or perhaps they become desperate because the organ they need is failing and they don't have long to live. Whatever the case, they end up buying the required body part on the black market. Even though it is illegal to harvest and sell these body parts, and illegal to use these parts in operation, it does not deter it from happening. The demand is too high. It is indeed a matter of life and death for some.

Of the 123,000 people in America on the list waiting to receive an organ, 100,402 of them are waiting for a kidney. There will only be 30,970 legal kidney transplants completed each year. The WHO reports that the rest of the people in need of organs will buy them off of the Internet, or die waiting.

An NBC news investigation found there were thousands of people living in Chicago, willing to sell their organs for money. They had even set up fake accounts that would advertise their organs on a website like Craigslist – they had been offered as much as $30,000 for one single organ.

Included in this investigation is the man known as the "Kidney Broker," Levy Rosenbaum. He was caught by the FBI selling three kidneys for a total of $410,000, after obtaining them from poor Israeli donors for only $10,000 each. There is supposed to be strict penalties for those that take part in trafficking body parts, including jail time and hefty fines up to $50,000. But in the Rosenbaum case, the sentence fell far short of this. He was only sentenced to 2 and ½ years in prison.

Chinese hospitals that are run by the state communist party are one of the most massive harvesters of body organs for trafficking. In 2006, in just one of their hospitals, they were exposed for trafficking 10,000 organs of prisoners, by force, which were sold for $1 billion. In the documentary "Human Harvest: China's Organ Trafficking," international investigators cite evidence that tens of thousands of people have been killed in China by Chinese officials to get the organs to sell. The Chinese communist party has denied all allegations claiming that neither transplant centers nor an organ-harvesting program exists.

In February 2016, television station "Al Jazeera" exposed a three-person organ trafficking ring in Indonesia. In the city of West Java, about 30 people had sold their kidneys for $5,000 each, while others had sold other parts of their bodies, such as their eyes for the corneas.

These terrifying stories don't just happen in third world countries as was seen in the Kendrick Johnson story. On January 11, 2013, the body of Kendrick Johnson was discovered inside a rolled-up mat in the gymnasium of Lowndes High School in Valdosta, Georgia, United States. Johnson was a student at the school, and his death was at first thought to be an accident.

The Johnson family didn't believe that their son died accidentally, so they had a private autopsy conducted on his body. From this, it was concluded Johnson died from blunt force trauma. During the private autopsy, it was also discovered that all of Kendrick Johnson's organs were missing. The funeral home had to stuff his body with newspapers to fill it up for the viewing of the body at the funeral. The police decided they would open an investigation into Johnson's death.

In 2014, Ryan Singleton, a 24-year-old man moved from his home in Georgia to California to pursue his acting career. His body was discovered in Death Valley with several of his organs missing. His eyes, heart, lungs, liver, and kidneys were gone. There were some who claimed it was probably some animals that ate his organs. Believable in those parts, only the rest of his body was intact and not torn apart.

In 2015, 24-year-old California State prisoner Nicholas Rodriguez went missing for more than 15 hours. He was found in a garbage can, with his body cut in half, and his organs were missing. Even though the prison had a security surveillance system, there was no footage of what happened to him on any of the cameras.

Is this where the future of organ trafficking is going? It would seem so. The papers and television news programs are becoming overcrowded with stories of people being kidnapped for their organs. In China, a missing 6-year-old boy was found alone in a field, crying as both of his eyes had been removed. In 2012, a young African girl was kidnapped and brought to the UK for the sole purpose of harvesting her organs. She was lucky because she was discovered before the operation happened. Police say they only catch a small percentage of these types of crimes.

In January 2004, Susan Sutovic of the UK received a phone call late one night awakening her from her sleep. It was a call from Belgrade, Serbia notifying her that her son, 24-year-old Peter, was found dead in his apartment. He was staying at her holiday apartment while studying Law. His roommate discovered Peter's body.

The paramedics were quick to the scene, and even though there was never a death certificate issued, the medical examiner classified the death as an overdose. His body was released and taken back home to Britain.. There was no official autopsy done on Peter, and the only evidence to support the overdose opinion of the medical examiner was a needle protruding from Peter's arm when the paramedics found his body.

Susan claimed to her knowledge her son didn't use drugs and was not an addict. Even ten years later, there still has not been a toxicology report released from the Serbian medical examiner. Susan also believed the death scene had been staged.

In Britain, a post-mortem exam was performed on Peter's body. It was discovered he had a high level of morphine in his body when he died, and there was no sign of any wounds. Peter's body was also absent of its heart and pancreas. Susan now believes that her son was a victim of organ traffickers.

"My son was murdered, but the Serbian and British authorities have put me through hell, forcing me to uncover the truth and blocking me all the way," says Susan to the UK Telegraph Newspaper. She thinks that he was either killed to get at her, and later they realized they could sell his organs for a large

amount of money, or he was just a victim of organ traffickers.

Susan's fear is not a case of a grieving mother in denial, who doesn't want to believe her son was an addict and would rather believe he was murdered. Amnesty International, British Medical examiners, and police officers all believe that Peter's death is highly suspicious. Susan hired two private investigators to review the evidence, perform tests at the apartment in Serbia, and see if they can discover something.

The detectives thoroughly examined the apartment where Peter died, and found blood in the bed where he died, in the kitchen, bathroom, and the hallways. They suspect there was a struggle. From the photographs taken by the Serbian police on the night of his death, Peter's face was covered in bruises, and he looked badly beaten. It turns out that the bed was soaked in blood. There was nothing in the photos that would support a simple overdose of morphine.

The detectives did further tests, one on the spoon found on the dresser table beside Peter's bed. The substance in the spoon was not heroin. The brown liquid was holy oil that came from Jerusalem. Peter always carried it around with him in a vial on a string around his neck.

Another of the tests discovered that the heroin in his bloodstream also contained the painkiller

Tramadol, which he had been subscribed and used since a car accident he had in the year 2000.

CHAPTER 3: LABOR TRAFFICKING

Labor trafficking is a form of modern-day slavery in which individuals are forced to perform labor or services through the use of force, fraud, or coercion. It also includes debt bondage and involuntary child labor. Labor traffickers use violence, threats, lies, and other forms of oppression to order to force people to work against their will. The most common examples of labor trafficking include people working as servants in homes, farm workers, and factory workers. They are usually forced to work in inhumane conditions, with no pay.

More often than we know, elements of forced labor are present in the supply chain of products and services we regularly buy. Human trafficking victims make an alarmingly high number of our consumer goods and food products imported to the United States. We, as consumers, and companies that subcontract cheap goods and services from traffickers, create the demand and incentive for these traffickers. Whether we realize it or not.

GOVERNMENT FORCED LABOR

A report by the National Immigration Justice Center states that over 48,000 people are being held in more than 200 immigration detention facilities in the United States. More than two-thirds are confined in facilities owned and operated by private companies working on contracts for the federal government. It has been reported that these privately run immigration detention centers are coercing detainees to work for one dollar per day, and if they do not work, they are punished.

The United States Congress needs to take control of this situation, and not just wait for lawsuits to free these people. The current administration has requested another $2.8 billion, so they can expand their detention holdings to 52,000 beds. This request should be rejected entirely. No government should be involved in forced slave labor let alone leading the way.

Even though the following is not the same thing at all, it is being used as a defense to this action. The American prison labor system, abolished years ago, still has one exception that allows prisons to require inmates to work without compensation. People who are detained while they wait for an immigration hearing are not prisoners. They have not been convicted of committing any crimes in society. Immigration is civil detainment, not criminal, and the people held should not be treated as prisoners. Under that law, only those convicted of a crime can be used for work, not even those just charged with a crime can be.

Under the Immigration and Customs En-forcement (ICE) Voluntary Work Program, immi-gration detention centers do not have to pay more than one dollar per day, for anybody detained for work they have done while in detention. This dol-lar per day rate was set by Congress in 1950 and has never been raised since.

The work program is supposed to be volun-tary. Detainees complain that if they ask for a day off, the staff members punish them by taking away essential items, such as toothbrush, toothpaste, etc. They also threaten to move them to a more dangerous part of the detention facility. Lawsuits are underway now, but they take a long time to process, which doesn't help in the day-to-day treat-ment of people wanting to immigrate to the US.

The following show examples of the punish-ment awarded to those refusing to work one day under a voluntary system:

1.   Wilhen Hill Barrientos was an asylum seeker from Guatemala, who was placed in CoreCivic's Stewart Detention Center in Geor-gia while he waited for his hearing. Late one night at about 2 a.m., Wilhen was awakened by a guard who wanted him to go to work in the kitchen. He was scheduled to work in the kit-chen at 10 a.m. that day. He told the guard he was too tired and wanted to keep his 10 a.m.

shift. The guard threatened to move him to the dormitory, an area riddled with violence and crime. So he submitted and went to work.

2.   Martha Gonzalez, from Mexico, and had been detained in the CoreCivic prison in Texas from May 2016 to August 2017, waiting for her T-1 visa granted to human trafficking victims. She regularly worked in the kitchen and laundry room. When she wanted to take a day off, the guard took away all of her hygiene items, including her toothpaste, and sanitary pads.

The CoreCivic responded by saying that the work program is entirely voluntary and that detainees are not disciplined whatsoever if they chose not to take part in it. The representative for GEO Group called the lawsuit's allegations baseless, saying that, "This is a strictly voluntary program and that the GEO Group provides hygiene products for free upon request."

In comparison, private corporations that own prisons in the US hold about 10% of the nation's prisoners. While private corporations have detention centers that contain more than 70% of the people in immigration detention. The government pays these private detention centers flat fees per person per day. In a privately owned profit-oriented system, the centers try and run their facilities as cheaply as possible by having the detainees cook their meals, clean, mop the floors, mow lawns, etc.

The revenue that an average facility brings in from the government is around $38 million per year. In 2017, the entire GEO group received $2.26 billion for all of their centers. Not only are these detention facilities getting money from the government, they in truth, charge detainees for their toiletries and personal necessities. They are not free upon request like they claim. It has been reported the average phone call is $12.75 for 15 minutes, a 4-ounce tube of non-flavored toothpaste is $11.

It should be stated that both the GEO Group and CoreCivic corporations asked to be the ones to house immigration detainees. In 2016 and 2017, CoreCivic spent $2.8 million in lobbying, and $700,000 in campaign contributions, while GEO Group spent $4.4 million in lobbying and $2.5 million in campaign contributions. Each of these companies donated $250,000 to Donald Trump's inauguration.

RELIGIOUS FORCED LABOR

Religion may be an area you never thought of or expected to see in the forced labor trafficking chapter. But in reality, it is a much larger problem than you could ever guess. It usually starts with people joining a church or religious group and investing everything they have, including their children.

The "United Nation of Islam" is a religious

group that was founded in Kansas City in 1978 by a man named Royall Jenkins. He is still the group leader, but now goes by the name "Royall, Allah in Person" and considers himself the 'Valued Creator.'

Kendra Ross, an ex-member, became a part of the church at a young age when her mother joined the group. Her life became public when she filed an $8 million lawsuit in federal court against the United Nation of Islam for unpaid servant and slave duties over 17 years. Ross lived and worked in the "Food for Life Supreme" restaurant in Dayton, Ohio, a restaurant owned by the religious group.

Her case was an example of human trafficking, not in the sex trade business, but trafficking all the same. This type of trafficking happens in plain sight for all to see, in large cities or small towns, and almost any kind of business.

Kendra Ross claims, *"I know what they are doing is wrong and they need to be punished for it and shut down. I mean, they took my childhood, my life and, I mean, I can't get that back. So, I want them to pay for that."* She described her average day to the court during her testimony.

"So, in the morning wake up, get myself ready, get the kids ready that were in the household, make breakfast, clean. And when the transportation would come, I would get the kids on the bus and then go to whatever job I was going to be doing. Mostly it was at the diner cooking. And I would do that until I went home. And when I

went home, there was more taking care of the children, cooking, dinner, cleaning and just basically took care of the household."

The Montgomery County Sherriff's office, the local FBI, and the Department of Justice offices all say that they had never received a complaint about the United Nation of Islam, or the restaurant. Even though Kendra Ross won her lawsuit, and was awarded $8 million in damages, there still has not been a criminal prosecution. Law enforcement claims that it's tough to get a witness to testify, as they are all members of the church or religious group. Without actual witness testimony, the case would be impossible to try. People that leave such a group lose everything, their friends and family, and therefore any help or support. So most are unwilling to testify.

Kendra Ross admitted that whenever someone wanted to talk with her, she wouldn't respond. She was terrified and too scared. Ross also told detectives that she had heard about other members that tried to escape, and they were killed. It wouldn't be until Ross was 21-years old that she would get the nerve to leave the group.

Sadly, the probability of Ross receiving her $8 million is slim to none. The group will probably close and claim bankruptcy, then reopen later under a new name in a new city, and start all over again.

FARM WORKER TRAFFICKING

Labor exploitation in agricultural areas is out of control according to the European Commission Report published in 2016. Countries like Portugal have a higher proportion of labor trafficking per one million of its' population than any other country in the European Union. Most of the victims in farmworker trafficking are men, and they are predominantly from Eastern Europe, India, Nepal, Pakistan, and Bangladesh.

Under such bad press, Portugal has decided to crack down on labor trafficking, and carry out thousands of raids on farms that are suspected of trapping poor migrants into unpaid work. The Council of Europe reported last year that labor trafficking in Britain, Belgium, and Portugal had overtaken sex trafficking in numbers.

Like many other things, Portuguese investigators say the usual victims are impoverished migrants that come to Portugal with the promise of a good job that is advertised on the Internet. Once they get to the position, the new employer confiscates their identity documents, such as passports, or driver's licenses. The workers are grouped in a shared room, where they will all live together. They will soon find out there is no pay for the work they will do.

In a recent article dated February 7, 2017,

on a farm in Portugal, police found 26 victims of labor trafficking. The farm workers were being used as slaves and worked for no money. In 2017, Portugal conducted 4,539 raids on farms, and other businesses like shops and services, to combat these crimes. They rescued a total of 175 people that were being used in forced labor.

Law Enforcement state that it is essential for outsiders to such groups to make reports if they see anything suspicious going on in any groups, even if they are under a religious title. They have started a human trafficking campaign called "Look Beneath the Surface" which was developed to bring awareness of this crime to the public. The known red flags that the campaign lists include:

1.   Untreated bruises or injuries of workers, or workers themselves being unclean or wearing dirty clothes

2.   Inconsistencies in stories about how much they work

3.   Failure to make eye contact with customers

4.   Looking scared, but still working hard

The most common places human labor trafficking is found in businesses include:

1.   Massage parlors

2.   Nail salons

3.   Strip clubs

4.   Escort services

5.   Youth door-to-door sales groups

6.   Construction companies

7.   Independently-owned restaurants and grocery stores

8.   Seasonal Farms, including fruit picking

The National Human Trafficking Resource Center has set up a hotline for reporting potential victims is 888-373-7888.

CHAPTER 4: MYTHS

In combating a crisis like human trafficking, it's critical to separate fact from fiction. This chapter is dedicated to exposing the incorrect information circulating about human trafficking. Here are some of the most common myths believed about human trafficking:

1. **HUMAN TRAFFICKING AND HUMAN SMUGGLING ARE THE SAME THINGS.**

Though these two terms are often used interchangeably, human trafficking is not human smuggling. Trafficking is the recruiting, transporting, harboring, or receiving of a person through force to exploit him or her for prostitution, forced labor, or slavery. Human smuggling is the transport of an individual from one destination to another, usually with their consent, for example across a border.

2. **MOST TRAFFICKERS ARE WHAT YOU SEE IN MOVIES OR TELEVISION.**

Most of the time the traffickers are portrayed as strong, gangster type people in movies and TV shows, but trafficking occurs in a wide range of classes, and they could be anybody, even your neighbor. In some cases, traffickers have been discovered to be politicians, police officers, business people, and even owners of restaurants.

While organized crime often plays a significant role in trafficking, local communities including their governments and even family members are often involved in the process as well. Many times it's just looked at as economics, and the people involved are not sick people. They think there is no other choice available to them.

3. HUMAN TRAFFICKING IS JUST PROSTITUTION

Human trafficking does not always mean prostitution. Quite often people are used for forced labor in everything from sweatshops making clothes, carpet factories, construction companies, farms, or housemaids.

4. ONLY WOMEN ARE TRAFFICKED

This seems to be the most widely believed myth I heard during the research on human trafficking. The truth is men and children are trafficked just as much as women. In fact, in the forced labor type of trafficking, men and children are trafficked the most. Farms and construction look primarily for men and teenage boys, as they can handle the heavy workloads far better than women do.

For sex trafficking though, it is still mostly women. But there has been substantial growth in the number of young boys being trafficked for sex in the last ten years. In some countries, young boys make up as much as 30% of the total people trafficked for sex.

5.   EVERY PERSON THAT IS TRAFFICKED HAS BEEN KIDNAPPED

In certain countries, when women respond to ads looking for waitresses or maids, they risk being trafficked. Placement agencies can confiscate their passports or any travel documents they carry and force them into working for nothing.

Oddly enough, there are times when people go willingly. They realize they are entering a job where they are going to be exploited, but they choose to go for the chance to make some money for themselves.

In the case of youths, sometimes it's a family or friend that recommends a job or opportunity in another country. The parent might send the child away, only for them to end up in a prostitution ring.

One of the biggest scams in youth trafficking is when parents are offered a sum of money to have their children sent to a country they think is better, as the United States. They are told the child will have to work off their travel costs, but then they will be free to live and work for lots of money in that country. This, of course, doesn't happen.

6.   TRAFFICKING ONLY HAPPENS IN THIRD WORLD COUNTRIES, AND NEVER IN

THE U.S.

While trafficking is something that does happen in many of the third world and poorer countries around the world, it also occurs in the U.S. According to the "Polaris Project," there are 100,000 to 300,000 children prostituted in America every year. The United States is the largest country to buy illegal organs from people trafficked for such a reason.

CHAPTER 5: GENDER, RACE & AGE OF TRAFFICKERS

According to the cases in the US District Courts up to and including 2015, 76% of the 293 defendants in slavery, forced labor, and sex trafficking cases were male, and 24% were female.

Concerning race, the defendants are broken down like so, White 20%, Black 60%, Hispanic 18%, Native American 1%, and Asian 1%.

The average age of the defendants was 27, with a significant number of those between the ages of 20 to 24 as well.

Below is a breakdown of the U.S. Department of Justice, Federal Prosecution of Human-Trafficking Cases for the year 2015, released last year in June of 2018.

TABLE 5
Characteristics of human-trafficking defendants in cases charged in U.S. district court, 2015

Characteristic	Total		Peonage, slavery, forced labor, and sex trafficking		Production of child pornography		Transportation for illegal sex activity	
	Number	Percent	Number	Percent	Number	Percent	Number	Percent
Number of defendants	964	100%	283	100%	370	100%	311	100%
Sex								
Male	849	88.3%	215	76.0%	341	92.4%	293	94.5%
Female	113	11.7	68	24.0	28	7.6	17	5.5
Race/Hispanic origin[a]								
White	515	56.9%	53	20.4%	271	77.0%	191	65.2%
Black	219	24.2	157	60.4	29	8.3	33	11.3
Hispanic	157	17.3	46	17.7	47	13.4	64	21.8
American Indian or Alaska Native	6	0.7	1	0.4	3	0.9	2	0.7
Asian, Native Hawaiian, or Other Pacific Islander	8	0.9	3	1.2	2	0.6	3	1.0
Age								
17 or younger	1	0.1%	1	0.4%	0	0.0%	0	0.0%
18–19	22	2.3	14	4.9	5	1.4	3	1.0
20–24	151	15.7	69	24.4	43	11.6	39	12.6
25–29	214	22.2	88	31.1	66	17.8	60	19.4
30–34	146	15.2	42	14.8	62	16.8	42	13.5
35–39	127	13.2	31	11.0	53	14.3	43	13.9
40–44	100	10.4	17	6.0	49	13.2	34	11.0
45–49	71	7.4	6	2.1	34	9.2	31	10.0
50–54	54	5.6	7	2.5	29	7.8	18	5.8
55–59	39	4.0	4	1.4	14	3.8	21	6.8
60–64	19	2.0	2	0.7	8	2.2	9	2.9
65 or older	19	2.0	2	0.7	7	1.9	10	3.2
Median age	33 years		27 years		35 years		35 years	
Citizenship								
U.S. citizen	896	93.9%	256	92.1%	355	96.5%	285	92.5%
Legal alien	28	2.9	13	4.7	6	1.6	9	2.9
Illegal alien	30	3.1	9	3.2	7	1.8	14	4.5
Education level								
Less than high school	182	22.2%	91	38.4%	52	16.5%	38	14.7%
High school graduate	280	34.6	77	32.5	121	38.4	85	32.0
Some college	242	29.6	58	24.5	89	28.3	95	35.7
College graduate	111	13.6	11	4.6	53	16.8	47	17.7
Marital status								
Single	419	48.9%	154	65.8%	142	43.2%	123	44.4%
Married or cohabitating	231	27.6	50	21.4	93	28.3	88	32.0
Divorced or separated	189	22.6	30	12.8	94	28.6	65	23.6
Criminal record[b]								
No prior convictions	477	49.5%	84	39.7%	209	56.5%	184	59.4%
Prior misdemeanor only	189	19.6	69	24.4	70	18.9	50	16.1
Prior felony conviction	297	30.8	130	45.9	91	24.8	76	24.5

Note: The unit of count was a defendant interviewed, investigated, or supervised by federal pretrial services. Percentages are based on nonmissing records. Data were missing for sex (2), race/Hispanic origin (59), age (7), citizenship (10), education level (146), marital status (126), and prior conviction (1).
[a]Excludes persons of Hispanic or Latino origin, unless specified.
[b]Includes both federal and state convictions.
Source: Bureau of Justice Statistics, based on data from the Administrative Office of the U.S. Courts, Probation and Pretrial Services Automated Case Tracking System, fiscal year 2015.

PART TWO: SURVIVOR STORIES

THE FOLLOWING ARE ACTUAL STORIES FROM AROUND THE WORLD BY THOSE THAT HAVE BEEN TRAFFICKED INTO SLAVERY

CHAPTER 6: I WAS A SLAVE FOR 40 DAYS

FLORA MOLINA - APRIL 5, 2011 (FORCED LABOR #1)

Flora Molina was living in a small town in Mexico when in the fall of 2001 her baby became ill. She didn't have any money so she couldn't afford to take her to the hospital. Sadly, her baby died. After her baby's death, Flora became severely depressed and became scared for what could happen to her other three children if they too were to get sick.

At a sewing class, her teacher approached her to tell her about a great job opportunity in the United States. There were no jobs where she lived, and minimal chances to make money, so she was very excited about the opportunity. Flora was told the position would provide her with a place to live, supply her with food, and when she got paid, she would be able to send money back home to her family. Flora jumped at the chance and took the job immediately. When she left for the US, she left her three children with her mother.

When Flora arrived in Los Angeles, she was picked up and taken to where she would be living. Her new 'boss' met her at the house and told her she would not be getting any pay to start. He said there was a charge of $3,000 for bringing her to the US that she would have to pay back first.

Flora was told she would be working in the garment district of Los Angeles making dresses. She says she worked 18-hour-days sewing dresses, and then she was expected to clean up the factory afterward. After her first day of work, Flora was told she would be sleeping in a room at the factory, and not going back to the house she was initially taken to when she arrived. She had to share a little room with another worker. They even had to share a single mattress thrown on the floor for sleeping.

There were other workers in the factory, but she was forbidden to talk to anyone. Flora was never allowed to leave the factory, or go outside. She claimed that during the whole 18-hour shift, she was only given one lunch break, that lasted about 10 minutes, to eat her only meal of the day. Flora said that she always felt hungry but worked hard. If she took longer than the allotted 10 minutes to eat, she was punished.

One of the regular employees, an American who was getting paid, noticed that Flora was always there, day and night. She started to become suspicious and thought there was something wrong with Flora. She approached Flora and handed her a piece of paper with her phone number on it. She told her that if she ever needed anything, she could call her anytime.

Flora was scared. She didn't trust anyone and remembered her boss telling her if she ever told anybody, or went to the police, her kids and mother would pay the consequences of such actions. Flora also figured the cops wouldn't believe her anyway, and she would probably just get arrested.

Her new life in the US went on like that for 40 days, which she said felt like 40 years. She began to feel sick every day, wondering how her children were. She wasn't able to call them and wondered what they thought happened to her. She hoped they didn't think she abandoned them.

Flora came up with a plan and asked her boss if she could go to a church to pray just once. After weeks of begging to go to church, she was finally allowed to go. When she arrived at the church, she immediately went to a pay phone and called the American co-worker that gave her the phone number. After she told the co-worker what was going on, she came and picked Flora up at the church. The pair went to a restaurant and talked about what the best thing to do would be. They both decided they would call the FBI.

An FBI agent put Flora in touch with a non-profit group called CAST (Coalition to Abolish Slavery and Trafficking), which found her a shelter to stay at, and gave her some necessities. She would finally regain her freedom, but there were still many challenges ahead of her. She would have to stay in America and testify against her trafficker, to avoid the charges for working illegally in the country.

The trafficker was charged and convicted, but only received a 6-month sentence of house arrest, where she had to wear an ankle bracelet. When she got out, the trafficker decided to come after Flora by threatening to hurt her family.

Flora said, *"I was enslaved for 40 days, but it felt like 40 years. Even though my enslavement doesn't define me as a person, it makes me who I am today. I am an advocate against slavery, I am a survivor of a crime so monstrous that the only way to move forward is to fight back. I am not the only one. There are other survivors that are fighting back with me. We are part of a group called the 'Survivors Caucus' and we are working to educate people, law enforcement and communities by using our stories. The caucus is a network of survivors where we feel safe and supported and we have advocacy to end slavery for good. Even though we were once victims we are now able to impact social change."*

Flora continues, *"If the big companies can show consumers, they are doing things to make sure the company is not using slave labor in the making of their products, these companies can be the key to freedom for hundreds of thousands of enslaved people. I know that from my experience even one person can make a difference. If companies post what they do to stop slavery, people will understand that they can buy from these companies and that will help stop the demand for these products."*

CHAPTER 7: VICTIM OF DECEPTION

VANNAK PRUM - JANUARY 2015 (FORCED LABOR #2)

Vannak Prum was living in Cambodia with his pregnant wife and was searching for an extra job that would cover the medical bill for the delivery of their new baby. One day he was out searching in town, a motorbike taxi told him that there was lots of work in Thailand, and he could even get him a job there drying fish.

At first, Prum felt suspicious about the job and decided to say no to the offer. But after a few months of searching for work and not being able to find anything, he changed his mind telling the taxi driver he would take the job. The taxi driver took Prum to Malai, where he joined 30 other men and women, who were then taken to Thailand on a bus.

In Thailand, the group waited until a large truck picked them up. He was crammed into the bed of the truck with the others, stacked on top of each other, and covered with a tarp. The group was taken to a small, windowless cement room, and locked inside. There was just one small hole in the wall that Prum could see out of, where he saw the ocean and lots of boats.

In the morning, Prum and the others were given clothing and taken on the boat, below deck, until they traveled far out to sea. Prum would spend three years on that fishing boat, enduring dangerous and grueling work for up to 20 hours per day, with almost no sleep. If any of the workers talked back or got tired, they would be beaten and tortured by the traffickers. Once, Prum himself was beaten with the tail of a stingray. He witnessed another victim be-headed by the captain in front of everyone.

The ship was at sea for three years straight. So, the first time it headed into a dock in Malay-sia to acquire a fishing license, Prum knew that he had to try and escape. He was very aware that if he got caught during his attempt, he could be beaten again, or even killed.

Prum and another slave jumped overboard late one night and swam several miles to shore, using empty fish sauce containers as buoys to help keep them afloat. They spent the first night in the forest, then made their way to a police station in the nearest town. The officers picked up the phone and made some calls before a red car came to pick them up.

The driver took them to a palm oil plantation in the jungle and left them there. They soon realized the police had sold them to work at the plantation. The plantation turned out to be a better place than the ship since they didn't feel so trapped.

One night, while the group was eating dinner, a fight broke out. Prum was slashed across his chest and collarbone with a knife. He was taken to the hospital to have his wounds treated, and for the first time since his capture, he had access to a phone. He phoned his home country officials in Cambodia, explaining what he had been through. When he was released from the hospital, the local police arrested him and placed him in jail.

Prum was taken before a judge, where the local prosecutor accused him of being an illegal immigrant and working in the country without permission. The police, not wanting to be exposed, lied at the trial, and Prum was sentenced to spend three months in jail. He would actually end up spending ten months there before being released on May 5, 2010.

Finally, after four years, Prum would be able to return home to Cambodia. He has made it his life mission to educate the people of the dangers of human trafficking by telling his story. On June 19, 2012, Prum was named a "Trafficking in Persons Hero," which is an honor from the Department of State, for his work in combating modern slavery.

CHAPTER 8: MY BOYFRIEND SOLD ME INTO SEX SLAVERY

SHAMERE MCKENZIE – JANUARY 2015
(SEX TRAFFICKING)

In 2005, Shamere McKenzie was a typical college student struggling with her tuition, rent, and paying her bills. She was living in Manhattan, New York, attending St. Johns University on a student-athlete scholarship. But after suffering an injury, Shamere was no longer covered. So she had to pay the remaining balance of her tuition herself.

It was during this time that she met a nice man while out at a club. The two of them became close quickly. He was very polite, very good at having stimulating conversations, and quite handsome. It was only a few months into the relationship when Shamere told him about her financial struggles with her tuition and bills.

The new boyfriend told her that she would save a lot of money if she gave up her apartment, and moved in with him. He said he wouldn't charge her anything for rent. Shamere accepted. Once she moved in, he told her she could make good, fast money if she would dance for clients. She knew other girls that had paid for their way through college by dancing for men, so she figured she would try it out.

The boyfriend bought Shamere new sexy dresses and shoes to work in and took her to a New Jersey strip club. He introduced her to the manager. He assured her she only had to dance, and there was never any contact with customers. Within a couple of hours dancing, Shamere made $300. She was excited that it wouldn't take long for her to make the $3,000 she needed to clear her debt.

A couple of weeks later, the new boyfriend

took Shamere to a party at a house in Brooklyn, where she offered to dance for some of the guests. While she was performing a dance for one of the guests, he demanded that she give him oral sex. She responded by yelling at him and calling him names. Her boyfriend quickly ran into the room, and instead of protecting her, he grabbed her by the neck and began choking her.

Shamere was shocked and told him she was prepared to dance for the men, but not have sex with them. The boyfriend punched her in the face, and she quickly fell to the floor. He kicked her a few times while she was there, and threatened to kill her family if she didn't do what she was told, or tried to leave. Shamere blacked out and didn't wake up until the next day. She found herself laying on the kitchen floor in a puddle of blood, covered in urine.

She began to cry, and the boyfriend came into the kitchen, apologizing to her saying he would never hurt her again. The next day when she got up and walked into the living room, he was slapping a young woman around. Shamere yelled at him to stop. He turned on her then, and beat her severely, leaving her in her bedroom.

It wasn't until the following month that Shamere was left alone in the apartment. She grabbed some of her clothes, escaping to her uncle's place where she decided she would stay. She started receiving threats from her boyfriend that he was going to hurt members of her family. After two weeks, she returned to the apartment, and was beaten, raped, and sodomized.

Shamere remembers, "*From the very first beating when I was choked to the point of unconsciousness until the day, he pulled the trigger on the unloaded gun in my mouth, I knew obedience meant survival. When he places the gun in my mouth and asked me if I wanted to die, I shrugged. I thought 'Finally this pain and this life would be over and the only one hurt is the one who is responsible for me being in this situation, me.' The trigger was pulled but I was still alive. For a few moments, I thought I was experiencing death with the ability to still see life, until I felt the blows to my head by the gun.*"

Because Shamere was afraid of her trafficker, she fulfilled all of his demands. Eventually, he would come to trust her again, and start to use her for other purposes. One of her new jobs was to drive the other girls he prostituted to different parties, and quite often the parties were across state lines.

On one of those trips, Shamere decided she could escape. When she took some girls to Dallas, Texas, she made her second attempt. After dropping the girls off at the party, she drove away thinking she wouldn't be coming back. But she couldn't go through with it and returned that same evening.

A few months later, when she took some of the girls to Miami, Florida, she approached some members of a Jamaican gang and asked them to help her escape. They agreed to help her and even kill her trafficker. However, when the attack was about to happen, she changed her mind. This upset the gang members, and they beat and raped her, dropping her off at her hotel.

Shamere decided that if she didn't make her quota for money, he would let her go. So, she started to see fewer clients. Her trafficker noticed and confronted her on how little she was making now. She told him that she wanted to leave. The trafficker agreed to let her go and even to give her $5,000.

After the agreement was made, he was getting the money, and she noticed him reaching for his gun. She ran out of the apartment. One of their neighbors saw Shamere running down the road screaming, so she got in her car and drove to pick her up. After she told her neighbor what was going on, they went to a hotel and called Shamere's mother.

At this point, Shamere didn't want to stay with her mother, or any other family, since she was worried her trafficker would hurt them. So, she ended up moving in with one of the girls who was also a victim of the trafficker.

In a sick twist of fate, they both ended up getting arrested for prostitution. The FBI also charged Shamere with transporting minors across state lines for illegal purposes. She spent three weeks in prison before being transferred to a program for victims of sex trafficking, where she received counseling and housing. She pleaded guilty to the "Mann Act," and was sentenced to five years probation, performed 200 hours of community service, and became a registered sex offender.

THE MANN ACT is a United States federal law passed in 1910 and named after Congressman James Robert Mann. The act made it a felony to engage in interstate or foreign transport of any woman or girl for the purpose of prostitution or debauchery, or any immoral purpose. Its primary stated intent was to address prostitution, immorality, and human trafficking, particularly where trafficking was for the purposes of prostitution.

After the cases were completed, Shamere began to work helping victims of sex trafficking at Courtney's House and began public speaking.

CHAPTER 9: MY FATHER SOLD ME INTO CHILD LABOR

JAMES ANNAN – JANUARY 2015 (CHILD LABOR #1)

James Kofi Annan was born in Winneba, Ghana. He was the youngest of 12 children, and none of his siblings were educated or had any type of schooling. His father sent the children away as soon as they were old enough to work, usually by the age of 6 years.

James remembers, *"I started my working life early, my parents had 12 children, none of them were educated. By the time I was six years old, I was the only person left in my father's control, all the others were older and most of them had already been given away to work, as I was the youngest, I was the only one still available.*

My father saw an opportunity and gave me away for fishing work. The way it works is that the person who takes charge of you now has control over you. I was first trafficked with 5 other children. Out of six of us, three lived, and three did not. I saw many children die from either abuse or the rigorous work they were obliged to do."

James told us about the type of work he was forced to do. *"I was forced to work excruciating hours catching fish on Lake Volta. On a daily basis, my day started at 3 a.m. and ended at 8 p.m. It was full of physically demanding work. I was usually fed once a day and would regularly contract painful diseases which were never treated as I was denied access to medical care."*

James was never allowed to take any breaks, and if he asked for some time off, they would beat him until he returned back to work. He claimed he wasn't allowed to sleep because he had so many tasks he had to take care of, such as mending nets and cleaning fish.

There were some times when he was able to see his mother. She wanted to take him back home, but that changed when James was moved to another fishing village too far away for his mother to come to see him. The only time he saw his father was when he was in the fishing villages to collect the money he and his siblings earned.

James had a deep desire to be educated, and

learn to speak English. This was what drove him to want to escape. More than the work and living conditions he endured. He tried to escape several times but was always caught. He suffered a severe beating each and every time.

Ten years into his captivity, the man he was named after died. It was customary for all people that were named after this man to attend his funeral. During the funeral, James was able to sneak away, jumping onto a bus that was headed to his home village. He was able to make it back to his parent's house. At the time, he was only 13 years old.

When he arrived home, his mother was happy to have him home. But his father was angry about the loss in income from James. His father wanted to send him back. It caused big fights between his parents, and eventually, it led to them getting divorced.

James' mother allowed him to enroll in school. He was laughed at but had such a deep desire to learn, that he didn't let it bother him. He was far behind his classmates, who already knew how to write. But he wanted to learn how to speak English more than anything else in the world. James ended up doing so well, with great grades, that he was chosen to attend college. *I went to the University of Ghana and took a job as a banker at Barclay's,* James exclaimed.

In 2003, James Annan started a program

called "Challenging Heights" which was created to help children get an education. Today, his program also rescues children who were enslaved in work villages like he was, and protects children considered vulnerable. He has received eight international prizes for his dedication and commitment to the education and protection of children.

CHAPTER 10: INDIAN CARPET INDUSTRY

RAVI SHANKER KUMAR – JANUARY 2016 (CHILD LABOR #2)

One of the largest industries using trafficked child labor is the carpet-making industry. In India's carpet making production, there are currently more than 300,000 children being used, and the majority of them are low-caste Hindu boys. The caste system in Hindu society is a system of hereditary classes distinguished by relative degrees of ritual purity, and of social status. The Hindu boys that are trafficked are called the 'Dalit' or untouchables and are considered lower than the lowest class in the caste. The carpet region in India is in Uttar Pradesh, which is a state in the northern-central region of the country.

Ravi-Shanker Kumar was one of those boys sold to the carpet making industry by his parents for a sum of money. Under the caste system, he would be worth nothing in common society. Ravi was forced to work 15-hour days, seven days a week, and received no pay. He was fed only one half a meal per day, was given almost no clothing, and quite often was whipped or beaten.

Kumar told 'Slavery Now' about his life during his carpet-making years:

'My name is Ravi-Shanker Kumar. I think I am between 12 and 13 years old. My cousin was working in the loom and it was he, in fact, who told my uncle to go back to the village and talk to my parents so they could send me there. My parents came up to me and asked me if I wanted to go. I refused. The loom owner refused to take no for an answer, however. They paid them a sum of 500 rupees ($10) and then, they asked me to leave. Once he paid the 500, the loom (the loom is a frame where the warp is tightened while making a carpet – it has two looms on the side, one on the bottom and one on the top. The size of the carpet is limited to the dimensions of the loom) owner and I took off from the village."

Ravi was put in front of a loom, and there was a mark made on the loom to indicate where he had to weave a carpet up to that day. If he didn't make it to that mark, he was left alone with just candle-light until he did get there. Most days, he was given so much to do; he would end up working late into the night, and he didn't get very much sleep. He was only fed once every day, at 12:30 p.m. But the food was usually half-cooked, and he had to force himself to eat it.

While working on the loom, it was usual for the children to get little cuts and nicks on their fingers. When they went to get a band-aid or something to put on the wound, the boss' wife would rub kerosene on the cut, and light a match to it, so that it would burn. They were then sent back to finish their weave.

If they only had a few cuts on their fingers, they were not allowed to stop working. They could only stop if the blood were running badly enough that it would get on the carpet they were making. In this case, they were beaten with one of the looms, or a punja (a type of loom that produces higher quality rugs). Most of the workers were only allowed one bathroom break per day.

Ravi only saw his father once after he was sent to the carpet-making factory. The loom owner wouldn't release him until he had finished the carpet he was working on that day. So his father ended up leaving without them speaking.

Ravi never tried to run away. The fear of getting caught was tremendous, and the loom owner always beat the children who attempted to escape. They were beaten so severely they were unrecognizable afterward. He was eventually rescued in a police raid and was taken to Ashram. There, Ravi

was given medical attention, counseling, and training to read and write.

CHAPTER 11: I WAS SOLD TO PAY THE RENT

DINA CHAN- JANUARY 2015 (SEX TRAFFICKING)

Dina Chan came from a very poor family that lived in a small village in Cambodia. She was sent to Phnom Penh to study in a cultural school. Dina was living with a different family but was unable to contribute anything for food or clothing. So they found her a job in a nearby hotel washing dishes. The hotel had sex workers that attracted many men. One night after work, Dina was on her way home, when a man attacked and raped her after following her from the hotel. She was only 17 years old.

After her attack, she was gradually lured into the sex trade business at the hotel. She was sent to the province Stung Treng and forced to have sex with men. If she refused, she was beaten. While she was working there, a man arrived and bought her for himself. He forced her to go with him. She was taken to a pig slaughterhouse where he worked and locked in a dark, smelly cell. At night after the men finished their work, they would come to the cell, and each one would rape her. There was always a minimum of 6 men each night.

In the morning, Dina lay in her dirty, dark cell, listening to the men herd the pigs. She heard them scream as they were being slaughtered. She wished the men would kill her too since it was likely her only escape from her nightly torture. She lived as a sex slave like this for six years before finally escaping.

In 1999, Dina spoke at the first National Conference on Gender and Development in Cambodia. She was able to help start, and is still a member of, the "Sex Workers Union of Toul Kork," and eventually became the Director of the Cambodian Prostitutes Union in 2006. Dina is still a sex worker now, but she and her sisters have demanded recognition of their humanity and respect. She now says, "*We are people, we are women, and we want to be treated with respect.*"

CHAPTER 12: WORKING AS A MAID

BEATRICE FERNANDO – FEBUARY 2014
(DOMESTIC SERVITUDE)

Sri Lankan Beatrice Fernando was 23 years old when she was divorced from her husband. She had to find a job to support her 3-year-old son and herself now that she was alone. Beatrice found an ad from a local employment agency looking for housemaids that could travel. Desperate, she took the job and was sent to Lebanon.

Beatrice remembers the day she was to fly out to Lebanon to go to her new job, *"I am at the airport in Columbo, Sri Lanka, saying good-bye to my 3-year-old son. With his eyes filled with tears, he asks, 'Can't I come with you, Mom? When you make a lot of money will you buy me a car to play with?' I take him in my arms, my heart breaking, and tell him, 'If I have the money, I will buy you the world.' My desperation to give him a better life has driven me to leave him with my parents, to go to Lebanon and be a maid."*

Beatrice was flown to Beirut airport, and taken to the job agent's office. When she arrived there, her passport was taken, and she was placed in a line-up with a group of about 30 other women. They all watched as small groups of 2 or 3 Lebanese men and women paced back and forth looking over the line-up of women, carefully examining their bodies, faces, and hands. Beatrice was finally sold to a wealthy woman, who took her to a beautiful fourth-floor condo building.

Beatrice was forced to work up to 20 hours per day. She was not fed, so she resorted to scavenging through the garbage to find food to eat. She tried to call the job agency, but the telephones were locked. She thought perhaps she could walk back to the agency, but all of the doors and windows were locked. When her new owner discovered she was trying to leave, she slapped her in the face and beat her until she passed out.

Beatrice became desperate enough that one day when she was outside on the fourth-floor balcony, she tried to jump to the ground and escape. As she stood holding the rail, a vision of her son went through her mind, and she asked God to help her survive. She slowly let go of the rail, and fell to the ground below, landing on her back.

Fortunately, Beatrice survived the fall and recovered at a hospital. Today, she lives in Massachusetts, United States. She continues to speak publicly about modern-day slavery, and she became the founder of "Nivasa Foundation," which is an organization that provides financial assistance for the education of trafficked women's children.

CHAPTER 13: MILITARY ENSLAVEMENT

ISHMAEL BEAH – JANUARY 2015 (MILI-TARY FORCED LABOR)

Ishmael Beah had a pretty normal life growing up, with an average family, and was interested in hip-hop. When he was 12-years old, he and his friends were performing in a talent contest in town a few miles away. While they were away, their hometown was attacked. Ishmael and his friends scrambled to get home as soon as they could.

When he arrived, he saw people running around the streets in a panic. Many were carrying their dead children, crying and screaming. Ishmael waited weeks for his family to appear, but they never did. They must have been killed in the attack.

With his home destroyed, family missing and safety at risk, he decided to leave. He and a few of his friends started traveling from village to village looking for food, water, and maybe some work. During his travels, he heard rumors some of his family were still alive, and they were taken to a nearby village. So he decided he would go there to look for them.

As Ishmael got closer to the village, he came across gunfire, smoke, and ashes. The whole village had been attacked and destroyed just like his home was. Only this time, he found his family members – killed and burned in one of the fires. At this point, a devastated Ishmael felt there was no longer any reason to keep running village-to-village. He decided to go to a village that was run by the government soldiers.

Ishmael liked his new home. There was plenty of good food to eat, soccer games to play with others, and a safe place to sleep. He didn't realize that by staying at the village, eventually, the soldiers would want something in return from him. He recalled the first sign of change, *"One day they just said, you know if you're in this village, you're gonna have to fight, otherwise you can leave. Some people tried to leave, but they were shot right in front of us."*

Ishmael continued, *"First, you know, you get your own weapon and everything and the magazines and the bullets, and then they give you drugs. I was descending into this hell so quickly, and I just started shoot-*

ing, and that's what I did for over two years basically. Whoever the commander said, 'This guy is the enemy,' there was no questions asked. There was no second guessing because when you ask a question and you say, 'Why,' they'll shoot you right away."

Through fear, indoctrination, cocaine, marijuana, and brown-brown (cocaine mix with gun powder), the government army turned Ishmael and other children into killing machines. He would later explain, *"What happens in the context of war is that, in order for you to make a child into a killer, you destroy everything that they know, which is what happened to me and my town. My family was killed, all of my family, so I had nothing. We had come to believe whatever our commanders were saying about how these guys didn't deserve to live, that we were doing the right thing and this group was the only thing that was slightly organized, and so, they become like a surrogate family in a weird way."*

Ishmael said it was his bond with a lieutenant that would end up rescuing and saving his life. That lieutenant was the one that would select people from the army, take their weapons away from them, and give them to the U.N. The lieutenant chose Ishmael. The UN workers took him and some other children to a rehabilitation center in Freetown.

Today, Ishmael advocates for war-affected youth and is a member of the Human Rights Watch Children Rights Division Advisory Committee and a UNICEF advocate for children affected by war. He has co-founded the Network of Young People Affected by War and started the Ishmael Beah Foundation which assists in the reintegration of war-affected youth.

CHAPTER 14: TAKEN

This next story is a horrific story about sex trafficking in the UK, by one woman who was kidnapped, raped, beaten, and forced into prostitution. Marinela was 17-years old and lived in Alexandria, a small town in Romania about a 2-hour drive from Bucharest. Sometime in mid-March 2008, while she was doing her homework in the apartment she shared with another female student, she heard a knock at the door.

Marinela answered the door to find two men standing there. One was Cornel, a man she knew from his reputation as a pimp, and the other was Marius Nejloveanu, someone she had never met before. They asked her if she would come to a barbecue. She refused saying she had homework due for the next day at school. Cornel went into a rage, and grabbed the back of her neck, slamming her head into the closet by her front door. *"Put your coat on!"* he demanded.

Marius saw her ID card and cell phone on the table near the television, grabbed them, shoving them in his coat pocket. She asked, *"Why are you taking my passport?"* He responded with only a cold stare. They forced her into their car and took her to the barbecue. Once they arrived, they gave her a drink and talked to each other quietly. Nejloveanu then forced her to go to another house that belonged to a relative of his.

There, she was raped. She cried and asked to go home. In response, they beat her until she was unconscious. Later when she woke up, there was a strange man in the room sitting beside the bed. Nejloveanu told her she had to have sex with him. After that, she was held captive in the house and wasn't allowed to go outside.

In the days that followed, her friends and family searched for her, but they had no clues as to where she went. Her school friends and teachers had not seen her and considered it strange that she would disappear. She was such a good student, and this behavior wasn't like her. When the search intensified, now with the police involved, her captors made Marinela a fake passport, giving her a new name, and a new date of birth saying she was 21-years old. They moved her to Bucharest initially, and from there, they sent her to the UK.

On April 3, 2008, Marinela arrived at the Birmingham central bus station, where a woman claiming to be Nejloveanu's girlfriend took her to a suburban house in Edgbaston. At the house, two other Romanian girls were living there. As she was unpacking her bag, one of the girls asked her if she knew how to put a condom on. She was surprised by such a question, and why they would ask it. The girls told her to get ready since they were going to a brothel. Marinela refused to go. Nejloveanu's girlfriend threatened her if she didn't go. She said that Nejloveanu would kill her as soon as he got there from Romania. Over time, Marinela became severely depressed, nervous, and jumping at every sound she heard. She was not eating, and she became very skinny, skeletal even.

Nejloveanu returned and gave Marinela a severe beating for not going to the brothel as she was told. She recalls, *"He beat me up and forced me to sleep with him and have anal sex. It really hurt. He was pulling my hair and hurting my back. Sometimes he would bang my head right on the corner of the door. That really hurt."*

After a few weeks of being raped and beaten every night, Marinela relented. Nejloveanu gave her a pile of sexy underwear, and she was taken to the nearby brothel that the other girls had tried to take her to earlier. She didn't speak any English, so she was unable to communicate with the clients, or say no to them. She wanted to tell the men that she had been trafficked, and was not there because she wanted to be. But none of them understood what she was saying.

On her first day, she made 300£, which would have been enough to support her whole family in Romania for six weeks. But she was not allowed to keep any of it for herself. Her day shift would last about 12 hours, usually from 10 a.m. to 10 p.m., every day. She would have sex with about 12 men on each shift for 40£ per man. Even though she was bringing in between 400-500£ per day, she would still have to ask if she wanted a cigarette, or cup of coffee.

Marinela explained it was hard to undress for the usually stinky men that she was forced to have sex with. Quite often, they were coming directly from work and hadn't showered. She found those to be the most disgusting. One of the men slapped her and pulled her hair, but nothing ever happened to the man. If he got too rough, they would take him outside.

The people that ran the brothel were ordered never to let her go outside, and she would some-times be there for days at a time. She tried to get out one time, and they beat her viciously and pulled some of her hair out of her head. After a few months passed, two more girls arrived from Romania. They were mentally challenged. Physically, they were 23-years old, but mentally, they were about 10-years old.

In October of 2006, Marinela was taken to Manchester to work in a massage parlor. Fifteen other girls were working there too.

It was in the early morning hours in May of 2009 when the police finally came to arrest Nejloveanu following up on a tip they received from the Manchester police. The Chief Commissioner,

Florea Stefan, said, *"Marinela is very lucky to be alive. Many of the girls are beaten very very badly, and there are still 7 girls that he exported to the UK, that have never been found. Trafficked girls are sometimes killed by their pimps everyone know that."*

Police extradited Nejloveanu's father, Bogdan from Spain, who was also involved in exporting girls from Spain to the UK for the purpose of selling them for illegal sex. Both men faced trial in Manchester, and both were convicted on 34 offenses. Bogdan was sentenced to 6 years, while Nejloveanu was given 21 years.

In February 2011, Marinela was finally returned to her parents in Romania. When her father found out what happened to his daughter, he attempted to burn down the house of Nejloveanu and had to be stopped by the police. Marinela didn't like being back home as she felt a lot of people thought she was now dirty and wished her dead. So, she traveled back to the UK, where she now lives. She has been training to become a hairdresser in Yorkshire.

Marinela estimated that overall she had worked with about 100 other Romanian girls who were all trafficked, and forced to work in the sex industry. Her account of the sex trafficking business in the UK proves how large off-street prostitution is there. In 2018, an investigation by police identified 5,890 brothels, saunas, and massage parlors used for selling sex.

An investigation by the Association of Chief Police Officers found that Marinela was one of 1,535 eastern European women working in the sex industry in the UK. There are some that say the true number is far higher than that. That estimate was derived from the places they've caught, and there are plenty of sex venues not yet discovered.

In the UK, some groups are complaining about the lack of police action against venues known to be selling sex illegally. Despite vast numbers of these brothels discovered, there is little evidence of police trying to close down these premises. An example of what happens to a place that does get caught in selling illegal sex is what happened with the "Shangri-La," whose owner was jailed after being convicted for running the brothel. But even though the Shangri-La was closed down, within one year, it reopened under the name of "Infinity," and even kept the same phone number. Its' website offers 36 girls, and when investigators called the establishment asking if the 30-minute rate for 40£ included sex, the receptionist answered, *"I can't say on the phone because it's against the law, but it does include a massage and full personal service."* It is estimated there are still between 50 and 100 people, both male and female, who are being trafficked every year in that area.

CHAPTER 15: STORIES FROM ICE

"The U.S. Immigration and Customs Enforcement" (ICE) recently released terrifying stories they've heard from some trafficking victims that were able to escape. The stories below are all true, but the names of the victims have been changed to protect their identities.

STORY #1: TONYA

Tonya was a victim of human trafficking used both for sex and labor services. Her story began when she was only 13-years old. She met a man named Eddie at the apartment building she was living in with her mother in the Dallas, Texas area. Eddie's estranged wife happened to be the property manager.

Tonya was in the same class at school as Eddie's stepdaughter, and the two girls would play together after school. She would often see him around the apartment building. One day the two girls were outside playing, Eddie introduced himself, and exchanged phone numbers with Tonya. Tonya said, *"It was a casual relationship at first. You could see there was a mutual connection. I thought he was cute, and I could tell he was really flirtatious with me. We would talk and flirt a lot, but it was not much more than that until I reached the age of 15."*

Tonya ran into Eddie one night at a local bar, and the two connected. She went home with him to spend the night. Tonya ended up running away from home and moved in with Eddie. At first, the two seemed to be in a normal relationship as a couple. He went to work, and she stayed home, looked after his younger kids once in a while, cooked, and cleaned for him.

Later, the two went to a party where they used drugs and were drinking. During that party, Eddie approached Tonya and told her to have sex with another man for money. Tonya felt very uncomfortable and told him no. He pressured her for about a half hour, telling her that if she loved him, she would do it. He also said it would only be this one time.

Tonya finally agreed to have sex with the man. But what she thought was only going to be a one-time thing, ended up happening almost every night for the next few weeks. Night after night and bar after bar, Tonya would go out with Eddie, who would advertise her to different men. She thought that she really loved Eddie, and it was all worth it to be with him. She would deal with the physical toll the trafficking took on her body, as well as the emotional and psychological effects, the hardest part. Tonya explained, *"Being able to sleep with that many people and live with myself and get up every day and keep doing it and just lying there being helpless was so hard."*

Help would eventually come for Tonya after police received a tip about Eddie's crimes. They passed it on to Homeland Security Investigator, Keith Owens, who would take over the case. Eddie pleaded guilty, and on May 25, 2015, was sentenced to 12 years in prison. During the trial, Tonya had to testify against Eddie, which was especially difficult, since she didn't know what the outcome would be, and whether he would be convicted or not. *"Telling people publicly about what I'd been through made me feel more ashamed because I'd never told anyone or was open about it."* Tonya said, *"The two special agents assigned to the case were the only two people I had really told everything to."*

Tonya feels her life is on a better track now, and she doesn't think about what she's been through much anymore. She doesn't want people to know. Her focus is only on moving forward now. *"I want to finish my GED and go to community college, take journalism, go to college and study political science and pre-law,"* Tonya claims. *"I just want to live a normal life, accept my past and not run from it."* Eventually, Tonya knows she will end up talking about her experience again. If she has children, she wants to be able to tell them about what happened to her so they will know what to look out for. Until that day, she still will pass on encouragement to anyone who may be experiencing what she did. *"You're worth something. You're very important to someone, no matter what he says, it's not true. You're worth something."*

The next two stories are first-person accounts of sex trafficking directly from the victim. Again, the names have been changed to protect the victim.

STORY # 2: LAURA

"I was around 17 when I met Robert. It started off with me and my friend meeting him for social purposes. It just went on for about nine months and we were living in different hotels the entire time and I don't even remember how many men there were. I was a runaway and wasn't living anywhere stable, so since I was underage most of the time, I sort of needed him in order to get hotels and move around."

"I had already been a prostitute since I was 15 and I think I just didn't even know what I was right or wrong and how should be treated. Towards the end, he held me against my will in a hostage situation and forced me to prostitute and took all the money and just beat me severely."

"The last time I saw him, he was just beating me until he was absolutely tired. I was covered in bruises; my face was completely disfigured, and it is causing me issue with my back to this day because of the way he was beating me and torturing me. That was probably the worst. There was a client in the room, and he was having an issue with something I couldn't do because I was all beat up. I didn't want to do it anymore. I didn't want to do anything. He wanted the money back. When Robert and he were talking I ran out of the room and somehow *was able to run faster than him."*

"I didn't tell anyone. I kept it to myself until I got a call from the FBI that he'd been arrested for something else and asked would I talk. Having to go face everything and realize how serious everything was. For the longest time I didn't even think it was that serious."

"At the trial, it felt empowering to look at him the entire time. I'm sure it drove him crazy. He can never touch me, but he had to look at me and listen and it made me feel good. "

"I had to learn that if I didn't at least have some kind of love and value for myself, no one ever will. My advice to other girls would be let people help you. It's not your fault and that you didn't deserve it. It's ok to be hurt about it because a lot of people will act like it never happened, because that's what I was going through."

Signed Laura 21

STORY # 3: APRIL

"I was 15 at the time and was a runaway. Tom wanted to be a pimp, so I would be in his room in his apartment and he would not let me go out for anything. He tried to intimidate me by threatening to beat me up if I tried to leave. I was scared of him so I wouldn't leave. He would drop me off at a hotel while he went to work."

"It lasted from March until June or July. Sometimes it would be every day; sometimes he would say, not today, but tomorrow. Out of the week, maybe 4-5 times a week, I was with different men."

"I just felt like that it was my fault and I deserved it, and nobody would ever believe me or try to help me, so I just let them control how I thought about myself. They were always verbally abusive and putting you down and it got to the point that I actually started believing it. Just letting someone control your own freedom take over just what you do. I couldn't leave the room. It was like wow, I'm letting someone make me feel scared."

"I never called the police because I felt it was my fault. I felt at the time like I had to stay. One day the FBI ended up coming to my house and contacted me because my name came up in their investigation."

"You have to know your self-worth. Its ok to ask

for help. They don't know they are a victim. They feel like its their fault. We are victims. You can have the worst past, but that doesn't mean you can't have a successful future."

Signed April 18

CHAPTER 16: FREE CYNTHIA

At 16-years old, Cynthia Brown ran away from home and moved in with her 24-year-old boyfriend. This is a familiar story. Only, her boyfriend was secretly a pimp that went by the name of 'Kut Throat.' By the time Cynthia realized that her boyfriend was not who she thought he was, it was too late. He forced her into a life of prostitution in the city of Nashville, Tennessee.

In 2006, Cynthia was picked up by a 43-year-old real estate agent, Johnny Allen, who took her to his place for sex. When the two were in bed, she thought he was going to kill her. He had reached for his gun that he kept in the nightstand. She panicked, jumped out of bed, and grabbed a gun she kept in her purse. She fatally shot Allen in the throat.

Brown was arrested, and charged with murder. During her trial, she told the court about how she was choked, beaten, and raped frequently in her home by several of the men she was forced to have sex with. On several occasions, she was threatened at gunpoint during sexual encounters. She was never paid directly for sex, and all the money went to her trafficker or pimp.

Brown was tried as an adult, and convicted of first-degree murder, felony murder, and aggravated robbery. She was sentenced to life in prison. Tennessee law had changed since Brown's conviction, where a person must be 18 or older to be charged with prostitution. Under that age, children are automatically considered a victim of sex trafficking in these types of cases.

Brown has recently argued her conviction, and life sentence was cruel and unusual punishment. In 2012, the Supreme Court ruled mandatory life sentences for juveniles without the possibility of parole are unconstitutional. But the U.S. District Court for the Middle District of Tennessee ruled that the 2012 decision did not apply to Cynthia Brown because she will be eligible for parole when she turns 69.

In 2011, a PBS documentary came out called "Me Facing Life: Cynthia's Story" that put Cynthia's case in the spotlight. Several celebrities have jumped on this case, speaking out to try and get her freed from prison. Kim Kardashian took up her cause and went to the White House to meet with President Trump about prison reform in May 2018. She was hoping to have the Brown case appealed.

"It's heartbreaking to see a young girl sex trafficked then when she has the courage to fight back is jailed for life! We have to do better and do what's right.

I've called my attorneys yesterday to see what can be done to fix this," Kardashian claims.

PART THREE: AFTER THE STORM

WHAT HAPPENS TO SURVIVORS
AFTER THEY'RE RESCUED?

CHAPTER 17: RETURN TO INNOCENCE

Most news outlets report on the great job law enforcement is doing in shutting down human trafficking, and rescuing victims so they can live a life of freedom. But is that what's really happening?

In October 2017, Denver news reported on the rescue of 84 children from sex trafficking. A teenager in California was also saved from sex trafficking. In 2018, we heard about 160 children rescued from another sex trafficking ring in Georgia. These are just a few of the hundreds of reports you can find browsing the many online news feeds, or reading the newspapers the old-fashioned way.

These rescues are excellent news to hear, and it is the right direction to be taking with the human trafficking issue that's going on in the United States, and throughout the whole world. After we hear such a report, most of us go back to drinking our coffee and return to work or daily life events. But for the people rescued and their families, this is only the first step. It is probably the easiest thing they are about to go through before returning to regular life again.

Most people think that if they have been rescued, everything is good, right? But most aren't aware of the time it will take to heal these victims. Currently, western medicine has devised a 3-phase, 9 to 12-month program set up in specific shelters for these victims to help them to get back into society.

PHASE 1

The first phase usually lasts about six months and is set up to help build a strong healing foundation that will help overcome the trauma of being victimized. One of the first things to address is the over-stimulation created from sexual and physical abuse. After long periods of constant abuse, a person's brain becomes overstimulated, stays on high-alert, and the victim cannot relax.

Similar to when a kidnapping victim becomes sympathetic to their captor, (i.e., Stockholm Syndrome), there's a comparable reaction with trafficking victims called "trauma bonding symptom." It's possible that survivors will feel sympathy or support for their trafficker. It may be an unconsciously feeling, so they don't even realize they think this way.

In this phase, survivors will be exposed to what is known as 'Equine Therapy' or 'Horse Therapy' - a form of experiential therapy that involves interactions between patients and horses. The victims become part of the daily activities of the horse (feeding, grooming, haltering, etc.). A mental health professional supervises this therapy and is guided by a horse trainer.

Both during and after the victims work with the horse, a therapist will evaluate and interact with them to identify their behavior patterns and help them process through their thoughts. The goal of the therapy is to help the victims develop, or redevelop, the skills and attributes they will need to function again in society, such as accountability, responsibility, self-confidence, problem-solving skills, and self-control.

Equine Therapy has been proven to help victims in the following areas:

1. Assertiveness

2. Emotional awareness

3. Empathy

4. Stress tolerance

5. Flexibility

6. Impulse control

7. Problem-solving skills

8. Self-actualization

9. Independence

10. Self-regard

11. Social responsibility

12.   Interpersonal relationships

Most of the success of this type of therapy is due to the nature of the animal. Horses are non-judgmental and have no preconceived expectation of the victim. Horse therapy has proven to help with any self-hate or self-blame for their circumstances. It also helps to build, or rebuild, their self-worth and confidence.

In this phase, survivors will also learn to establish healthy life rhythms, such as waking up and going to bed at the same time every day, exercising regularly, and doing their own grocery shopping.

PHASE 2

This phase is started sometime during the Phase 1 process, usually around the 3-month mark, determined by the therapist. During this phase, the everyday life routines of a victim's life are reconstructed. One of the critical parts of this therapy is for the victim to get back their personality, and regain the things that make them an individual. Most victims are stripped of these things by their trafficker to train them to follow commands without question, and from trying to escape.

They will be given a cash budget and bank account to help teach them how to manage their money again and responsibility. They will be educated from whatever point they had stopped at the time of their kidnapping. So, some will get their high school diploma via GED, while others will take college courses. Another important thing is for them to get health coverage, and to be treated for any medical condition they might have as a result of their captivity. The most common in trafficking victims is dental care.

When the survivor feels they are capable of living on their own, and the therapist is comfortable with such a move, they will begin to look for housing and employment. These are usually the most difficult things to achieve. The Federal housing project has a long waiting list because of overcrowding. Employment can even be harder than finding housing. Many trafficking victims end up with a criminal record like what was described in some of the previous stories, even if they were trafficked into prostitution against their will, or they were forced to commit some crime under duress. There are also logistical challenges such as transportation to search for a job, and then how to get there each day once a job is secured.

PHASE 3

The third and final phase is usually not mandatory for the survivor to complete. It can be done while they are still staying at the shelter, or have moved into their housing. This part of the therapy is the part where the survivor is fully functioning as an adult in the world. They are responsible for managing all aspects of their lives from work, rent, paying bills, and even preparing to date someone. This last phase is more like providing a support system to help them while they are adjusting to their new lives.

These are the typical phases for a survivor of human trafficking. But there are also other things a victim is left to deal with that is not included in shelter therapies, like the potential consequences of physical or medical issues. Victims often end up with malnutrition, or pregnancy, or even diseases such as AIDS. They could also have been forced into, or just fell into, an addiction with alcohol, narcotics, and other drugs.

In the case of managing a sexual disease, they have to be treated with drugs and receive more counseling, especially if it's a chronic condition that could kill them such as AIDS. Most of the shelters are not equipped to handle these cases. So, in addition to the Equine therapy, they will have to seek further care

In the case of pregnancy, if they decide to have the baby, it quickly adds an element of stress on them. The responsibility attached to their lives can be very overwhelming since they are still trying to cope with their other issues. Again, these shelters are not equipped to handle such things, and the survivor usually decides to go the adoption route.

Most of the female victims that became pregnant during their time in captivity have had an abortion. They may have had several abortions.

This tends to lead to problems in the future if they get married and want to have a family.

The drug and alcohol treatments have to be handled outside of the shelters as well. Usually, they are sent to local AA groups, as there is little to no cost to the patients.

CHAPTER 18: HOW TO RECOGNIZE & REPORT HUMAN TRAFFICKING

"Hope for Justice," a non-profit organization, gives us the general indicators of what to look for in *people that might be trafficked*:

1. They may be fearful of police, or other authorities

2. They might be afraid of the trafficker, believing that their family member's lives are at stake if they were to try and escape

3. They exhibit signs of physical and psychological trauma, such as anxiety, loss of memory on recent events, bruising, or an untreated medical condition

4. They will be fearful of telling others about their situation

5. They may be unaware that they are being trafficked, and think the job they are doing is just a really bad job to have, or think that all workers are treated the way they are

6. They will have very limited freedom of movement

7. They are probably unpaid or given just enough to barely survive

8. They will have limited or no access to any medical care or treatment

9. They seem to be in debt to someone else

10. They have no passport even though they are from another country, or say that someone else is holding onto their passport

11. They may be moved regularly to avoid detection by law enforcement or immigration agencies

12. They may be controlled by some sort of witchcraft or superstitious ways

It is also important to be aware of any *hotels or houses that seem to be used* for sexual activities. Victims being trafficked and used for sexual exploitation may:

1. Be moved between cites or hotels quite often

2. Be sleeping at the same premises that they are working at

3. Always have the same clothing on, or not have very many outfits, usually one or two, and can be very provocative in nature

4. Have a regular substance abuse issue, or even be addicted to drugs

5. Be forced or intimidated into providing

sexual favors to others

6.   Be subjected to abduction, assaults or rapes

7.   Be unable to travel freely, or are always picked up and dropped off by the same person or using the same vehicle

8.   *Have the money that they earn from their services collected by someone else*

Forced labor used in criminal activities such as marijuana-growing operations may be noticed by:

1.   The windows of the property always covered from the inside

2.   People visiting the property at unusual times, or late at night

3.   Being at a residential home

4.   Unusual noises coming from the property, like machinery

5.   Pungent smells coming from the property

Domestic Servitude usually has a particularly serious form of denial of freedom to the victim. Things you might notice include:

1.   The victim lives and works for a family in a private home

2.   They do not eat with the family they work

for

3.	They have no bedroom or proper sleeping area for themselves

4.	They have no private space at all

5.	They are forced to work excessive hours, even up to 24 hours at a time

6.	They are never allowed to leave the house without the employer, or owner of the house with them

7.	Are malnourished

8.	Are reported as missing, or accused of a crime by their employer if they tried to escape

In the case of *child abuse* by a person of power or trust, exploiting that position to obtain sexual services in exchange for something like alcohol, drugs, attention or gifts, you may notice a child that:

1.	Often seems to go missing, or truant in school, etc.

2.	Is very secretive

3.	Has unexplained money or presents

4.	Is experimenting with drugs or alcohol to take away their stress

5.	Is associated with, or being groomed by older people, that are not in their normal networks

6.   Are in a relationship with significantly older people

7.   Are taking part in social activities with no plausible explanation

8.   Are seen entering or leaving vehicles of unknown adults

9.   Are showing evidence of physical or sexual assault including having STD's

10.   Show signs of low self-esteem or image, perhaps self-harming or has an eating disorder

IN THE UK, concerns should be reported at

(T) 0300 008 8000, or

(E) info.uk@hopeforjustice.org

IN THE US, concerns should be reported at

(T) 615-356-0946, or

(E) info.us@hopeforjustice.org

CHAPTER 19: TATTOO YOU

ATTENTION CALLED TO TATTOOS USED
DURING SEX TRAFFICKING

In Wisconsin, sex trafficking survivors and their lawyers are now working across the state to bring attention to a new sign of exploitation – the branding of a sex slave worker with a tattoo. The tattoo is probably not what you think it would look like. It's not a picture of something, but more like a barcode, you would see on products found in your grocery stores.

Nancy Yarbrough, a survivor, started the Milwaukee non-profit group called "Fresh Start Learning," which provides resources to women and children who are victims of sex trafficking. Yarbrough told Wisconsin Public Radio that tattoos are commonly used now in the sex trade to show that a person belongs to a specific trafficker. In Wisconsin alone, FBI reports indicate the number of commercial sex trafficking offenses recorded in that state nearly doubled, from 34 to 59, in 2017. The following image is what a sex trafficking tattoo looks like:

PART FOUR: TRAFFICKERS GET CAUGHT

WHAT HAPPENS TO THE TRAFFICKERS?

CHAPTER 20: PROSECUTING TRAFFICKERS

According to the United Nations Office on Drugs and Crime (UNODC), the first of many things needed to capture and convict human traffickers is the cooperation of every country's government and their police forces. Most often, things go wrong when everyone is not on board. In some countries, traffickers are caught and arrested, prosecution brings charges against them, but then corrupt police officials end up releasing the identity of the victims and witnesses to the traffickers. Once that happens, the victims or witnesses are intimidated out of testifying, or they go missing. It always ends up with the trafficker released, and the charges dropped. UNODC is trying to prevent this by helping establish effective law enforcement in these countries.

UNODC has also helped to develop legislation in these countries as well. Many countries have minimal human trafficking laws if any. They also do not have much in the way of assistance for the victims of trafficking. Some of these country's laws are so limited in scope because many sweatshops are operating in their country, and there is an incentive to keep them in business. Their own country's officials want to continue to make money off of them. Without specific human trafficking laws, victims are subjected to considerable uncertainties, while traffickers face little chance of any real penalties.

So far, UNODC has completed drafting new anti-human trafficking legislation in Armenia, Lebanon, and South Africa. They have also been allowed to train police departments in Burkina Faso, Ghana, Nigeria, Togo, Ukraine, and South Africa. They are currently working in the West and Central African countries. UNODC is also spending time training police officers, border guards, prosecutors, judges, and NGO staff in Afghanistan, Burkina Faso, Finland, Ghana, Laos, Moldova, Nigeria, South Africa, Ukraine, and Vietnam.

PROSECUTION IN CANADA: EVE - A TRUE STORY

In 2008, a man named Imani Nakpangi pleaded guilty in an Ontario, Canada court for the trafficking of a Canadian minor by exercising control or direction over her movements for the purpose of sexually exploiting her. He was the first person convicted of a human trafficking offense under the Criminal Code in Canada. He was also charged with living off the avails of prostitution, related to another girl who was a 14-year-old ward of the Children's Aid Society at the time.

Court records show that the victim, called 'Eve,' was under Nakpangi's control for three years. Eve tried to leave him several times, but she was chased, threatened, and assaulted by him. He also threatened to kidnap Eve's brother, and sell him as a sex slave unless she worked long enough to pay him a $100,000 'Exit Fee.'

Eve had a work log that she kept, which showed that she worked virtually every day, and turned over about $360,000 to Nakpangi. Eve escaped one night when one of her clients robbed her at gunpoint. Afterward, she went to the police instead of back to Nakpangi's home. When the police raided Nakpangi's house, they found a younger girl there as well, who claimed she loved Nakpangi and was carrying his baby.

WHO ARE THE TRAFFICKERS?

To run a successful sex trafficking operation, many people must be involved. So, when they get caught, it's not just the hands-on pimp being sued over the crime any longer. In February 2019, the Albuquerque Journal reported that a woman who was sold for sex when she was still a teenager, was now suing the Albuquerque Motel 6 where the trafficking occurred, and the now-closed Backpage website that advertised her services. Her lawsuit claims that both businesses had a part in allowing her to be trafficked.

The lawyers who filed the suit have already filed 20 similar lawsuits to this one in Texas, but this is the first one to be filed in New Mexico. They claim that they are trying to shine a light on the many different ways human trafficking can flourish. One of the attorneys, Annie McAdams, said her legal team doesn't intend to agree to a settlement. *"Our Jane Does were the ones that we choose to file on, who are doing this for more than just money,"* McAdams explains. *"We are looking for a significant disruption in the status quo in the human trafficking and hospitality world."*

Since January 2018, McAdams and her co-counsel, David Harris, have filed numerous cases alleging hotels, trucking companies, and even Facebook facilitates sex trafficking or at least failed to recognize clear signs of someone being trafficked. They have also filed numerous suits against Backpage. Their first case will go to trial in April 2019.

McAdams said their latest case, filed in the Second Judicial District Court in Bernalillo County, involves a woman from a suburban area in Albuquerque, only identified as Jane Doe #17. McAdams claims the woman was only 17-years old when she fell in love with a man who said he was her boyfriend, and then trafficked her at different locations around the city from the years 2013 to 2014. One of those locations was the Midtown Motel 6 on University NE near the Big L in Albuquerque.

The suit alleges the motel had a duty to exercise reasonable care in discovering that the danger of human trafficking, as well as the trafficking of Jane Doe #17, occurred or was likely to occur at the Subject Motel. It claims the motel failed to properly train staff to look for signs of human trafficking, failed to prevent traffickers from renting a room, and didn't install security devices that could have helped deter or identify human traffickers.

"The evidence is pretty strong for that hotel knowing what was going on due to the frequency of the visitors to the room," McAdams said. *"As well as that, she was a minor and was brought on the premises by somebody that didn't register as a guest."* Motel 6 did not respond to questions or requests for comments.

This same motel made the headlines in 2017 when a man was shot to death in one of the rooms because of his alleged connections to a sex trafficking ring. Federal authorities said 39-year-old Daryl Young had been killed by a hitman who was hired by a married couple running a sex trafficking ring. Police said Young, and trafficking victim Tobi Stanfill, were killed at the direction of Cornelius Galloway because their activities were contrary to the objectives of the criminal sex trafficking organization. The case is pending in federal court.

Much of Galloway's business relied on posting advertisements on Backpage.com according to the court records. Jane Doe's lawsuit states that Backpage would sanitize advertisements, taking out certain words that would point to underage sex trafficking, like 'Lolita', 'School girls,' 'Innocent' and 'Amber alert.' Backpage was aware that their website was used for the advertising, selling and sexual exploitation of young women, including Jane Doe #17. Despite this knowledge, Backpage refused to take reasonable steps to prevent the trafficking of Jane Doe #17, and other similarly situated young women. Backpage CEO, Carl Ferrer, pleaded guilty to conspiracy to facilitate prostitution, and money laundering.

Seven other officials were charged in federal court, and their cases are still pending, according to the court records. McAdams said the story isn't over yet, and the lawsuit seeks compensation for medical expenses, non-medical expenses, pain and suffering, and attorney fees. *"There are still extraordinary harms and losses caused to this population, and Backpage should be held accountable,"* McAdams claims. *"So, we have not ceased our efforts against them."*

INTERNATIONAL SEX RING TAKEN DOWN IN THE US

In December of 2018, the federal government of the United States handed down convictions for 36 defendants for their roles in a massive international sex ring, with 5 of the leaders going to trial. The sex ring was based in Thailand, which sold women in several U.S. cities, including Minneapolis, where they were tried. At a press conference, the officials said that this was the largest sex trafficking ring ever dismantled by the federal government.

The U.S. Attorney for the District of Minnesota, Erica MacDonald said, *"Sex trafficking is an industry that is built on supply and demand and the organization fed that industry. It exploited, it abused, enslaved, and sold women in response to the high demand of commercial sex that exists not only in the United States, but in Minnesota."*

The operation started in 2014 after police received a tip about the activity going on in Minnesota. The victims were all women in their thirties, who were smuggled in from Bangkok, Thailand. They were all sold in cities throughout the states including Minneapolis, Los Angeles, Houston, Chicago, and Washington D.C.

The U.S. attorney said that the women were sold like cattle until they could pay off a bondage debt. The operation had been going on for more than a decade and generated tens of millions of dollars for those involved. There were hundreds of victims and thousands of men who purchased these women. Police claim that many of the women who were victims were misled to believe that participating in the scheme would lead to a better life.

According to MacDonald, it was an organization that brought poor and vulnerable women from Thailand to the United States where they were forced to engage in sexual acts, every day, all day, and they couldn't walk away. Many of these victims are now working to rebuild their lives, and the primary defendants in the sex ring will face sentencing sometime this year.

ICE ARRESTS NEARLY 2000 HUMAN TRAFFICKERS IN 2016

In 2016, the U.S. Immigration and Customs Enforcement (ICE) and the Homeland Security Investigations, arrested 1,952 people for human trafficking, or illegal trade and exploitation of people for commercial gain, most commonly in the form of forced labor, and commercial sexual exploitation. From those cases they rescued over 400 trafficking victims, and provided them with critical services. This was the highest number on record of people arrested.

Nine years ago, in 2010, the President of the United States, Barrack Obama, declared January as the National Slavery and Human Trafficking Prevention Month. And in that year, ICE arrested 300 people for trafficking. The number almost tripled in 2011, to 938. The year 2012 stayed about the same with 967 arrested, but 2013 saw it nearly double again to 1,877. The year 2014 saw 1,770 arrests, and 2015, the number dropped to 1,437. But in 2016, the numbers soared again to 1,952.

Sadly, of all the people arrested for human trafficking, only half of them were convicted.

HUMAN TRAFFICKING CONVICTION DETAILS IN CANADA

In Canada, the province of Ontario has 65% of all the human trafficking cases in the country. However, the conviction rate is still only around 7% of those arrested.

According to the Toronto Police, the annual statistics for trafficking are:

- 2013: Occurrences-67, Arrests-11, Charges -70, Victims-14

- 2014: Occurrences–149, Arrests-59, Charges-365, Victims-33

- 2015: Occurrences-170, Arrests-61, Charges-463, Victims-30

- 2016: Occurrences-136, Arrests-52, Charges-330, Victims-30

Source: the Toronto Police Service, Sex Crimes – Human trafficking Law Enforcement

WHY IS CONVICTION RATE OF TRAF- FICKERS SO LOW?

According to the UNODC's 'Global Report on

Trafficking in Persons' released in 2014, impunity remains a serious problem. 40% of the countries recorded few or no convictions, and over the past ten years, there has been no discernable increase in the criminal justice response to this type of crime. This lack of convictions leaves a significant portion of the population vulnerable to offenders.

The report highlights that almost all countries in the MENA region (the Middle East and North Africa, with a current population of 381 million people) have laws against human trafficking, but they do not enforce them. It is the UNODC's opinion that these countries do not have the training or workforce to ensure a proper investigation, prosecution, and adjudication of trafficking cases. These countries also do not have any interest in pursuing a rights-based approach towards the trafficking victims.

The report claims that the biggest concern in the MENA region is child trafficking, with 62% of their victims, children. Most of the victims in that region are Asian, followed by Sahara Africa, and 35% are females trafficked mainly for labor.

In America, of the 1,513 prosecutions conducted, there were only 946 convictions, with 8,821 rescued victims. Most of the cases don't get a conviction because there is usually a lack of witnesses. Either the trafficked workers get deported, or they go into hiding and don't show up for trial. In some cases, the witnesses are threatened by the traffickers or their associates, and they end up not testifying.

PROTESTERS AGAINST TRAFFICKING IN BERLIN, GERMANY, OCTOBER 2018

Despite an increase in the number of trafficking victims in Europe, the number of convictions has fallen by a quarter. The United Nations (UN) reported that 742 people in Europe were convicted of trafficking offenses in 2016, compared to 988 in 2011. The number of victims increased from 4,248 to 4,428 in the same years.

According to Kevin Bales, a professor of contemporary slavery at the University of Nottingham, the fall of convictions reflects a couple of things - the hardening of border controls across Europe, and a failure to recognize victims of abuse. *"People who might have been detected as victims of a crime in the past in a lot of western European countries, are now being treated as not victims of a crime but as illegal migrants and are being deported or dumped that way,"* Bales explains.

The drop in the number of convictions is also because of the new difficulties set by new slavery laws. Bales explains,*"The convictions either are hard to make, and we know that to be true, under some of the newer slavery and trafficking laws, or they are choosing to prosecute under a statute with which they are more likely to get a successful prosecution."*

For example, prosecutors are now opting to pursue convictions for crimes such as grievous bodily harm, because the evidence is easier to get and therefore much easier to prove. The other problem with these types of convictions is that the traffickers are not convicted of trafficking, and when released, they are free to do it again.

The UN report also warns that more countries are now experiencing some form of violent conflict than any other time in history. Armed groups use trafficking as a strategy, and are exploiting and abusing people to show they have control over the community. Or they are increasing their forces, by recruiting children soldiers or giving sex slaves as a reward for their recruitment.

The UN report further states that for the first time the majority of victims are people trafficked in their own country. It is now about 6 of 10, and again could be because of the stricter border controls.

Alan R. Warren

EPILOGUE

January has now been proclaimed National Slavery and Human Trafficking Prevention month by the Department of Homeland Security in the US. It is a time to help make all people aware of the signs of human trafficking, and where to report suspected instances.

The Blue Campaign's "Wear Blue Day" is on January 11 in the US, and it's a day where everyone can show their solidarity with the victims of human trafficking by wearing blue and raising awareness about these crimes. The idea is to bring trafficking out from the shadows, and into clear view of everyone. Hopefully, this will prioritize the issue, and help communities, and countries, to band together and bring a stop to trafficking.

Polaris, a non-profit organization that contracts with the U.S. government to run the National Human Trafficking Hotline, has been collecting data since 2003, and they have identified over 22,000 victims of trafficking in the United States alone. From these victims, the Department of Justice has now federally prosecuted over 900 human trafficking cases.

HOW MANY HUMAN TRAFFICKING CASES ARE IN YOUR STATE?

The darker the state's color, the more cases reported. California, Texas, and Florida stand out in particular on the map.

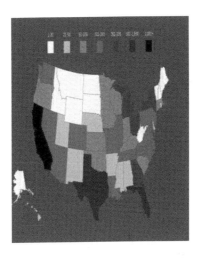

MAP OF THE STATE-BY-STATE REPORTED CASES OF HUMAN TRAFFICK-
ING ACCORDING TO THE NATIONAL HUMAN TRAFFICKING HOTLINE

ABOUT THE AUTHOR:
Alan R Warren

Alan R Warren, PhD, has written several Best-Selling True Crime books and has been one of the hosts and producer of the popular NBC news talk radio show 'House of Mystery' which reviews True Crime, History, Science, Religion, Paranormal Mysteries that we live with every day from a darker, comedic and logical perspective and has interviewed guests such as Robert Kennedy Jr., F. Lee Bailey, Aphrodite Jones, Marcia Clark, Nancy Grace, Dan Abrams and Jesse Ventura. The show is based in Seattle on KKNW 1150 A.M. and syndicated on the NBC network throughout the United States including on KCAA 106.5 F.M. Los Angeles/Riverside/Palm

Springs, as well in Utah, New Mexico, and Arizona.

Beyond Suspicion: Russell Williams: A Canadian Serial Killer

#1 Bestselling Book in True Crime Depositions

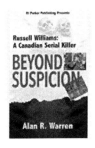

Young girl's panties started to go missing; sexual assaults began to occur, and then female bodies were found! Soon this quiet town of Tweed, Ontario, was in panic. What's even more shocking was when an upstanding resident stood accused of the assaults. This was not just any man, but a pillar of the community; a decorated military pilot who had flown Canadian Forces VIP aircraft for dignitaries such as the Queen of England, Prince Philip, the Governor General and the Prime Minister of Canada.

This is the story of serial killer Russell Williams, the elite pilot of Canada's Air Force One, and the innocent victims he murdered. Unlike other serial killers, Williams seemed very unaffected about his crimes and leading two different lives.

Alan R. Warren describes the secret life including the abductions, rape and murders that were unleashed on an unsuspecting community. Included are letters written to the victims by Williams and descriptions of the assaults and rapes as seen on videos and photos taken by Williams during the attacks.

This updated version also contains the full brilliant police interrogation of Williams and his confession. Also, the twisted way in which Williams planned to pin his crimes on his unsuspecting neighbor.

Amazon United States
Amazon Canada
Amazon United Kingdom

Deadly Betrayal: The True Story of Jennifer Pan - Daughter from Hell

Find out what really happened when seasoned true crime reporter and author, Alan R. Warren, takes you through the details as they unfold in this book of a Deadly Betrayal.

A family of three tied up, each with a gun to their head. "Where's the money? Where's the fucking money?" one of the intruders yelled. A petrified daughter tortured and forced to listen to her parents being shot in cold blood. "I heard shots, like pops," she told the 911 operator, "somebody's broke into our home, please, I need help!" Was this a home invasion? Or something else, more sinister, a Deadly Betrayal.

The real-life horror story that happened inside the Pan family home shocked their normally peaceful upscale Toronto neighborhood. The Pans were an example of an immigrant family. Hann and his wife, Bich Pan, fled from Vietnam to Canada after the U.S.-Vietnamese war to find a better life. Their daughter, Jennifer, was an Olympic-caliber figure skater, an award-winning pianist, and a straight A student.

The Pans worked their way up in this rags-to-riches story, now living in a beautiful home with luxury cars in the driveway. Was it these expensive items that lured three intruders with guns into their home on the night of November 8, 2010?

Amazon United States
Amazon Canada
Amazon United Kingdom

View ALL BOOKS by the Author at:

https://www.amazon.com/Alan-R.-Warren/e/B01LG8S48Y

ABOUT THE AUTHOR:
RJ Parker

RJ Parker, PhD, is an award-winning and best selling true crime author and owner of RJ Parker Publishing, Inc. He has written over 30 true crime books that are available in eBook, paperback and audiobook editions and have sold in over 100 countries. He holds certifications in Serial Crime, Criminal Profiling and a Ph.D. in Criminology.

To date, RJ has donated over 3,000 autographed books to allied troops serving overseas and to our wounded warriors recovering in Naval and Army hospitals all over the world. He also donates to Victims of Violent Crimes Canada.

OTHER BOOKS BY RJ

Parents Who Killed Their Children: True Stories of Filicide, Mental Health and Postpartum Psychosis

Serial Homicide: Notorious Serial Killers: (4 Books in Series)

Abduction

Top Cases of the FBI: Volumes I and II

The Basement

The Staircase

Forensic Analysis and DNA in Criminal Investigations and Cold Cases Solved: True Crime Stories

Serial Killers Encyclopedia: The Encyclopedia of Serial Killers from A to Z

Social Media Monsters: Killers Who Target Victims on the Internet

Escaped Killer

Revenge Killings

Killing the Rainbow

Marc Lépine: True Story of the Montreal Massacre: School Shootings

Backseat Tragedies: Hot Car Deaths

Women Who Kill

Beyond Stick and Stones

Cold Blooded Killers

Case Closed: Serial Killers Captured

Radical Islamic Terrorism in America Today

Hell's Angels Biker War

Serial Killer Groupies

Serial Killer Case Files

Blood Money: The Method and Madness of Assassins: Stories of Real Contract Killers

Serial Killers True Crime Anthologies: Volumes 1 – 4

CONTACT INFORMATION

Author's Email:

AuthorRJParker@gmail.com

Publisher's Email:

Agent@RJParkerPublishing.com

Website:

http://RJPARKERPUBLISHING.com/

Twitter:

http://www.Twitter.com/realRJParker

Facebook:

https://www.Facebook.com/AuthorRJParker

Instagram:

https://Instagram.com/RJParkerPub

Bookbub:

https://www.bookbub.com/authors/rj-parker

Amazon Author's Page:

rjpp.ca/RJ-PARKER-BOOKS

REFERENCES

1. *https://www.nytimes.com/topic/subject/human-trafficking*

2. *https://www.nytimes.com/2012/04/19/opinion/kristof-not-quite-a-teen-yet-sold-for-sex.html?rref=collection%2Ftimestopic%2FHuman%20Trafficking&action=click&contentCollection=times-topics&region=stream&module=stream_unit&version=search&contentPlacement=10&pgtype=collection*

3. *https://deadspin.com/heres-what-to-expect-next-in-the-robert-kraft-case-1832833904*

4. *https://www.nbcnews.com/news/us-news/what-happens-foreign-human-trafficking-victims-united-states-n770041*

5. *http://netnebraska.org/article/news/1141911/how-backpage-shutdown-impacted-commercial-sex-industry-and-trafficking*

6. *https://bigthink.com/philip-perry/what-you-need-to-know-about-human-organ-trafficking*

7. *https://www.psychologytoday.com/ca/blog/reading-between-the-headlines/201311/body-snatchers-organ-harvesting-profit*

8. *https://www.telegraph.co.uk/news/uknews/10146338/Organ-trafficking-a-deadly-trade.html*

9. *https://gizmodo.com/heres-how-much-body-parts-cost-on-the-black-market-5904129*

10. *http://www.medicaltranscription.net/*

11. *https://humantraffickinghotline.org/type-*

trafficking/labor-trafficking

12. *https://www.nytimes.com/2019/01/29/ opinion/forced-labor-immigrants.html?rref=collection %2Ftimestopic%2FForced %20Labor&action=click&contentCollection=timestop- ics&region=stream&module=stream_unit&version= latest&contentPlacement=4&pgtype=collection*

13. *https://www.ajc.com/news/national/labor- trafficking-victim-hidden-plain-sight-working-dayton- restaurant/V4MYM4LugvSsNdwOS5wnCP/*

14. *https://www.washingtonpost.com/news/ monkey-cage/wp/2019/01/11/young-black-men-are- disproportionately-likely-to-be-prosecuted-for-human- trafficking-this-explains-why/? utm_term=.ec4dc1bb0bf7*

15. *http://www.endslaverynow.org/blog/articles/ flor-molina*

16. *http:// thecnnfreedomproject.blogs.cnn.com/2011/04/05/i- was-enslaved-for-40-days/*

17. *https://www.crchealth.com/types-of-therapy/ what-is-equine-therapy/*

18. *https://fightthenewdrug.org/what-happens-to- sex-trafficking-survivors-after-theyre-rescued/*

19. *file:///C:/Users/al%20warren/AppData/Local/ Microsoft/Windows/INetCache/IE/G8HNBAPH/ trends-in-housing-problems-and-federal-housing-as- sistance.pdf*

20. *https://www.unodc.org/unodc/en/human- trafficking/prosecution.html*

21. *http://www.governing.com/topics/public-*

justice-safety/tns-Cyntoia-Brown-tennesee-sex-trafficking.html

22.   *https://www2.gov.bc.ca/gov/content/justice/criminal-justice/victims-of-crime/human-trafficking/human-trafficking-training/module-2/case-study-2*

23.   *https://usiaht.org/news/?gclid=EAIaIQobChMIt4uak-zo4AIVryCtBh3vhQQMEAAYAiAAEgJvl_D_BwE*

24.   *http://www.fox9.com/news/36-convicted-in-largest-international-sex-trafficking-ring-brought-down-by-federal-government*

25.   *https://aplus.com/a/annalisa-enrile-human-trafficking-website?no_monetization=true*

26.   *https://www.ice.gov/news/releases/ice-arrests-nearly-2000-human-traffickers-2016-identifies-over-400-victims-across-us*

27.   *https://www.ice.gov/features/human-trafficking-victim-shares-story*

28.   *https://qz.com/1171897/i-was-a-victim-of-sex-trafficking/*

29.   *http://craigslistconfessional.com/*

30.   *https://www.theguardian.com/uk/2011/feb/06/sex-traffick-romania-britain*

31.   *https://www.theguardian.com/global-development/2019/jan/08/trafficking-convictions-fall-25-despite-rising-number-of-victims-in-europe*